Transformation:

From Lost in the World
to Found in the Lord

by First Lady Cassandra Peters

Published by BOTR Press, LLC

Poplarville, MS

© 2020 by Cassandra Peters

Published by BOTR Press, LLC

Poplarville, MS 39470

Cover portrait courtesy Cassandra Peters

Interior photos courtesy Cassandra Peters

Cover photograph by Sebastien Gabriel on unsplash.com

Cover graphics by Catherine Bolden

Unless otherwise indicated, all scripture is King James Version.

ISBN: 978-1-7347101-0-6

Transformation:

From Lost in the World
to Found in the Lord

by First Lady Cassandra Peters

Table of Contents

Foreword

Welcome to the messages of a woman who has walked through the valley of the shadow and come out into the sunlight of God's love on the other side.

First Lady Cassandra Peters has a heart for the Lord and a gift for sharing her passion through her words. I've listened to many preachers and teachers over the years. Few of them leave me filled with holy fire and a renewed desire to be the woman God wants me to be like Cassandra does.

In the years I've known her, I've watched her grow from wonderment at the Lord's calling to confidence in speaking his message. She offers insights into God's faithfulness based on her own struggles and supports her conclusions through scripture. Cassandra is not afraid to share her trials and stumbles along the way. Her transparency provides others with guidance on their path and gives them hope that they, too, can achieve a closer walk with God.

I've found inspiration and renewed direction through reading these messages. I believe you'll also be blessed by your time spent with a lady I'm proud to claim as my sister in the Lord, First Lady Cassandra Peters. Come in with an open heart and you will be filled.

Yours in Christ,

Mary Beth Magee
Christian Author and Speaker
www.LOL4.net

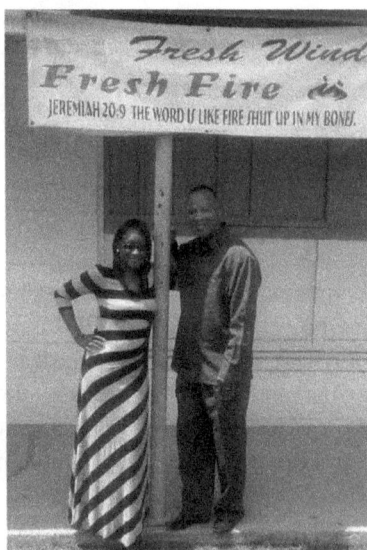

First Lady Cassandra Peters and
Pastor Jimmy Peters

Acknowledgements

First, of all I thank God who is the head of my life, for allowing me to write this book, which has really helped me to have an even closer walk with him. He gets all the praise and glory.

Secondly, I thank God for my kids Trevon, Isaac, Matthew, and Jasmine and I thank them for encouraging me to continue to write when I felt like stopping.

Thirdly, I thank God for my husband, Pastor Jimmy Peters. His Godly leadership of our household helps me to walk and grow as a Christian. God sent me the righteous man I needed, just when I needed him.

Again, thanks to you all and may God Bless all of you.

First Lady Cassandra Peters

Introduction

Hello, my name is Cassandra Ducre Peters,

I was born in Honolulu, Hawaii; but I currently live in a small town with many people called Poplarville, Mississippi. I have four lovely kids, three boys and a girl. Their names are Trevon, Isaac, Matthew, and Jasmine. I love them so dearly. They have been an inspiration to me. When I felt like putting down the pen, God used them to push me to do what he wanted me to do and that is to finish writing this book.

I've been a single mother. I have been down. I have been hurt. But God brought me through.

I decided to write this book to encourage everyone: the hopeless, the lost, the unsaved and the saved, and all God's chosen children. While writing this book my life started to change for the better. I was even encouraged myself with the words God has led me to write down in this book.

Sometimes we have to encourage ourselves when we are in our lonely state. There is nothing wrong with that, my friend. When God hasn't sent someone to give you a boost on your way, remind yourself of his promises. Just know that God sees and hears you. The struggles will soon be over after a while.

First Lady Cassandra Peters

The Beginning of the Journey

First Lady Cassandra Peters

Chapter 1: Being Used by God

In the year 2007 I gave my life over to the Lord. I would not have it any other way.

I am not saying I am perfect; no one is perfect. The word of God says, "For all have sinned and come short of the glory of God" (Roman 3:23). However, I do follow all the commandments found in the Old Testament of the Holy Bible (Exodus 20). These commandments were given directly by God to the people of Israel at Mount Sinai after He had delivered them from slavery in Egypt. But I learned there was more to obeying God than just following the old rules.

Preparing myself for the things of God

After many nights of fasting, laying at the altar before my father and reading God's word increased my spiritual understanding (Philippians 4:7), knowledge (Proverbs 18: 15), and wisdom (Proverbs 3:19-20, James 1: 5), God has allowed me to tap into his glorious presence. While in God's presence on December 18, 2009 he revealed to me a lot of things that were going to come to pass in my life.

This put me in mind of when God came to Joseph in a dream and told him he would someday rule over all his brothers and even his father (Genesis 37). Joseph was his father's favorite, which caused his brothers to become very angry with him. Joseph had no idea that his brothers would become so jealous of him. He was just being his own loving self, carrying on with his daily duties.

Sometimes the enemy tries to sneak in and ruin your day when you are not paying him any attention, but when you have the favor of God all around you nothing can hinder what God has for you.

Joseph brothers had no idea that one day all the mean things they were doing to their brother would come back to them, causing them to be subject to the one they envied so much. We need to watch how we treat others, because that very same person can become our boss one day. That's how it happened with Joseph and his brothers. They did wrong to him in his youth, but he rose above them in the end.

All my life I have been talked about, pushed to the side and called "weird," and people said I would not amount to nothing or nobody. But God had other plans for my life in spite of my enemies. In spite of my setbacks I was always important to God. He saw the best in me when everyone else around me only saw the worst in me. He never gave up on me.

A Great Move of God

God revealed to me in a dream that I would preach his word, and lay hands on the sick and they would recover, just like he said in Mark 16:18. As months went by God gave me many visions on what he wanted to do through me.

One morning during the summer time in 2010, God opened a door for me, so I stepped out on faith and believed what he has been telling and showing me for the last couple of years. I'm reminded in God's word when it says, *"I can do all things through Christ which strengtheneth me."* (Philippians 4:13)

It tells me here that God is my strength, and if I abide in him, and his words abide in me, I can ask whatever I will, and it shall be done for me (John 15:7). That day I was a little nervous. After reminding myself what the word of the Lord said brought comfort to my spirit, I proceeded in the name of Jesus.

First let me tell you before I get started when you are handling God's business you have to "deny yourself" (Matthew 16:24) and follow God's plan. Self will get in the way and mess up your part in the plan of God and his works that he has assigned for you to do at that moment. That is why fasting and seeking the face of the Lord is a must when doing the work of the Lord, because you will be held accountable for your actions.

If he tells you to do something in someone else's life, and you don't do it, you are guilty. Don't let their blood be on your hands (Ezekiel 3:18).

"God is not a man, that he should lie; neither the son of man, that he should repent: hath he said, and shall he not do it? or hath he spoken, and shall he not

make it good?" (Numbers 23:19) God spoke it and it sure did come to pass.

On a hot summer morning about 8:00 a.m. in 2010 I was working with this young man who is autistic. He worked at Winn Dixie (a grocery store in our town). My job was to make sure he stayed focused on his job and did it the correct way. For example, things like bagging the groceries correctly and bringing buggies in from the parking lot. I took my job seriously. There came a time when he was outside collecting buggies. I was keeping an eye on him and I saw this young lady that worked in the Deli department at Winn-Dixie walking like she was in pain.

As she walked towards me, I asked her what was the matter. She told me she got bitten by a poisonous spider on her left leg. I really was not thinking about praying with her or laying hands on her on at that time, but in my mind, I was praying for her.

The next day as she begins to get out her car and walk toward me. I notice that she was walking even slower. The closer she walked toward me the hotter my right hand was getting (felt like it was on fire) and I heard the voice of the Lord say, "Lay your hands on her."

I started a conversation with her by asking her, "how big is the bite?" She said it was as big as five quarters put in a circle, with a lot of infection in it.

I asked her, "Do you believe in the power of prayer?" She said yes. God then gave me the opportunity to pray for her.

Picture this: I'm standing in front of the soda machine in front of Winn Dixie focusing my mind on God. I laid my right hand on her right thigh and started praying in the name of the Lord Jesus. As I was praying, I could feel the healing power of God taking place.

The heat from my hand drew out all the infection from her leg as I finished praying for her. I was so weak from the energy that God allowed me to use on her behalf I could hardly stand up. She was crying and said her leg was so hot and she also said she received it in the name of Jesus. Come to find out her father pastors a church. I said, "Look at God in the right place at the right time. "

As she proceeded to go clock in, God told me to tell her within two to three days she would be healed. God told me to tell her instead of the healing taking place from the outside, it was going to start from the inside out, and then she would be completely healed.

A week and a half went by before I saw her again because I was on vacation. I saw the young lady at work, and she said "Cassandra, I cannot believe how you were so right. I was healed in two days," she said. "There is no scar or anything."

I said, "Thank Jesus, you showed up right on time." What a Mighty God we serve!!!

Often time people look at me because I "look young with so many kids" as they quote, it used to bother me, but now I got used to it. I am reminded in the word of the Lord in Isaiah 26:3, *"Thou wilt keep him in perfect peace, whose mind is stayed on thee: because he trusted in thee."*

Children of God, this is the time and the hour for us to put our trust in God. Man will disappoint you and try to destroy you. The enemy's job is to steal, kill, and destroy us (John 10:10). As long as you are a child of God, the devil will try to destroy you.

He sees your future. We all have greater days ahead of us if you only have Faith as small as a mustard seed (Luke 17:6). God will honor just that small a bit of faith.

On the other hand, God will give you strength and build you up in the midst of what you are going through. I am a witness. Many times, I found myself getting weak, but God has always been there to lift me up.

Be careful about what decisions you make and choose your friends wisely. This flesh is very easy to be distracted. Ephesians 6:12 tells us our struggle is not against flesh and blood, but against the rulers, against the authorities, against the powers of this dark world and against the spiritual forces of evil in the heavenly realms.

I really did not understand in the beginning, but when God started to open doors for me to use my gifts it seemed like the whole world was caving in on me. The Bible says, *"When the enemy shall come in like a flood; the Spirit of the LORD shall lift up a standard against him"* (Isaiah 59:19). I thank God for lifting up a standard against the enemy for me because I should have been dead and gone sleeping in my grave. But I thank God for his Grace and Mercy that is still keeping me alive today (Exodus 34:10-11). He has made a covenant with me, so that he can manifest himself in me and through me.

Chapter 2: Growing in His Word

Let's continue on my journey of Gods healing power being manifested through me.

Early one cool fall morning in 2010 I was assisting my client in bagging groceries and collecting buggies in Winn Dixie parking lot when I spotted one of my friends, who worked in the meat department. He was sitting outside on his break, so I decided to go talk to him. I approached him on his left side and said hello to him.

He stated, "If you're talking to me, I cannot hear you. My left ear has been stopped up for the last two weeks with drainage."

I asked, "Have you gone to the doctor yet?"

He said, "No I need to make an appointment today."

As I was standing there my left hand felt like it was on fire, so I asked him, "Do you believe in the power of prayer?"

He answered, "I can always use some prayer."

So, God led me to put my hand on both his ears. My hands were getting hotter and hotter. I kept on praying until I felt the release of the Holy Spirit.

My friend jumped a little and said, "My ear popped." It popped two more times, then God allowed me to be released and by the power of Jesus he was healed instantly. The pain went away, and he could even hear. He was amazed and said, "Thank you."

I said "I give God all the Glory, because when God use you as a vessel, you can take no credit for what he has done." God is a jealous God (Deuteronomy 6: 15) and he also trusts those whom he blesses with gifts to use their gifts properly. Mark 16:17-18 states *"And these signs shall follow them that believe; In My Name shall they cast out devils; they shall take up serpents; and if they drink any deadly thing, it shall not hurt them; they shall lay hands on the sick, and they shall recover."*

I have come to let someone know that God is still in the blessing business. God knows what we need, when we need it and who needs it. God is an on-time God. He will never leave his children hanging (1 Samuel 12:22). If God said it, it shall come to pass, but in his timing (Ezekiel 12:25).

Often time we get discouraged because some of us are impatient. It reminds me of myself. Seems like the more we want something to happen the longer we have to wait. You know it's coming but not sure when. While waiting. we keep asking God, "Hello, God. It's me can you hear me" and God is saying, "Just a little while longer."

If he gives it to us right when we ask for it, we will never acknowledge that it came from God.

That's just like if my kids want money and if I just give it to them, they will have in their mind that they don't have to work for it or wait for it like their friends. "All I have to do is ask."

If I just give it to them that means they haven't put any work in their chores or schoolwork or whatever the situation may be. I'm saying today is while you are waiting for God to open some doors for you, just praise and thank him as if he has already done it. All God wants you to do is acknowledge him in everything you do and ask for. (Proverbs 3:6).

On one particular morning when I woke up the Holy Spirit was heavy on me, so I did praise and worship all morning while getting the kids ready for school, even in the car. So, when I got to my daughter's Head Start school where she was going at that time, I was still praising and worshipping.

I walked her into her classroom to sign her in. I notice one of her teachers was standing behind the door with her hand on her head. I asked her, "What is the matter?"

She said she had a bad headache.

I asked her, "Do you want me to pray for you?"

She said, "Sure."

So, I laid my hands on the front and the back of her head and prayed and she said, "I feel chills going through my whole body."

I said, "That's the power of the Holy Ghost."

She was healed instantly. God is so awesome, he also works in mysterious ways by his wonders God performs in our everyday life.

For example, one evening the kids and I were on our way in the house from playing basketball in the back yard. We were trying to figure out what we were going to have for dinner, knowing we did not have any food left.

I started to pray out loud and said, "Lord, you said you will make a way out of no way. Me and my kids do not have any food and any money. Can you please come help us?"

My daughter and son started repeating the prayer that I said. As we were praying, we walked in my room. I called to check my food stamp card which had a zero balance. As I started to leave the room, out of nowhere my oldest son said, "Mommy, why don't you look in that purse hanging behind your door?"

I answered him, "That purse is old and has been hanging there for at least two years." Still, I took his advice and looked in it.

I pulled out old receipts, pens and all of a sudden, I saw a wrinkled-up bank envelope. In it were two one-hundred-dollar bills. The kids and I were amazed, and I started crying with happiness and praising the Lord.

That is how I know that God works in mysterious ways. What a treasured memory. What an amazing testimony. I know if God did it for me, he can and will definitely do it for you! God is an on-time God!!

After reading and searching and praying and even asking different preachers, teachers and reachers about the goodness of the God I just decided to find out for myself. Even though God was using me in a spectacular way to touch those around me, I still had many questions about God.

I am reminded in his word when he stated in Matthew 7: 7-8, *"Ask, and it shall be given to you; seek, and ye shall find; knock, and it shall be opened unto you; For every one that asketh receiveth; and he that seeketh findeth; and to him that knocked it shall be opened."*

When God reminded me of those scriptures, I knew that there was more for me to know about the goodness of God. I came to realize no matter how much God reveals to me, I will never as long as I live find out all there is to know about him, God is just that wonderful. Just like the church folks say if I had ten thousand tongues, I could not thank him enough, why? Because God is just that good!!

Chapter 3: Another Day's Journey to Success

As I continued my journey to seek the Lord and to know more about him, I looked in the best place, the place where I know that the truth lays: in the Holy Bible.

I am reminded that in Matthew 19:29 Jesus states that "...*and every one that hath forsaken houses, or brethren, or sisters, or father, or mother, or wife, or children, or lands, for my name's sake, shall receive a hundredfold, and shall inherit everlasting life.*" God is not saying give up on everything going on in your life. He is simply saying that "I gave you houses, cars, kids and money etc. only for your fleshly pleasures; but if you don't take those things for granted that which I have blessed you with and seek me first, I will make sure you have ever lasting life."

The first few times I read this passage, I asked myself how a person could stay focused on God and not the things that they can enjoy and see. After all, you cannot "see" God.

However, I continued my journey to know more about God. I did some searching on the internet, checked out books from the library and checked into many other sources. I came to realize I have been searching in the wrong places. The only way I can find out more about God is if I pray and fast and seek him for myself and continue to read my Bible. Often times it is so easy to lose focus when you are seeking God's face. The enemy throws distractions at us.

For example, the kids start acting up, the phone rings, the dog won't stop barking. It could be any various kind of distraction. You just have to sacrifice some time to spend with Jesus even if it just ten minutes.

Every minute spent with God is precious to him, you just have to gradually work your way up to spending more time with him. Remember, God is a jealous God according to his word found in Deuteronomy 6:15. God does not want to be second in your life, he wants to be first, God wants all the glory because he allowed his only begotten son Jesus Christ to die on the cross for you and me.

We find ourselves complaining about the little things that don't even matter. Can you picture in your mind, giving your one and only son's life up for someone else to live? Then that same exact person that you allowed to live turns their back on you, denies you, talks bad about you, and puts your name to shame? How would you feel. I know if that was me, I would feel disgusted, used, wasted in my efforts, etc.

But I thank God his thoughts are not like our thoughts and his ways are not like our ways (Isaiah 55: 8-9). Sometimes we find ourselves complaining and really have nothing to complain about. I challenge you today to start appreciating the small things in your life and let God know that you appreciate him allowing his son Jesus Christ to die on the cross for you. Because if it was not for the goodness of the Lord who is on our side each and every day, every breath we take where would you be?

Some of us should have been dead a long time ago, but I thank the Lord each and every day for making a way out of no way. When I couldn't see my way out of being alone, being broke almost being homeless, when I felt like I was going to lose my mind, didn't have nothing to eat for me and my kids, car broke down, kids acting up, my so-called friends turning their back on me and my family talking about me, he made a way. I thank God every day for his strength, for his Holy Ghost power. Because I know that *"I can do all things through Christ which strengtheneth me"* (Philippians 4:13).

That means no matter what issues come up on you in your life, God said you can do all things through him. I challenge you this day forth to follow Proverbs 3: 5 and put all your trust in the Lord and don't rely on your own understanding. Don't lean on your money, house, car, kids, mom, dad or self, but lean on God. He will take care of you, God's Word is true and full of promises, and God's words do not and will not come back void (Isaiah 55:11). God does not make empty promises.

Just open up your mouth, your heart and ask God to walk with you, talk with you, to be your comforter.

I know many have heard that saying, a closed mouth doesn't get fed. So how do you expect to walk in the fullness of God if you're not letting him know that you appreciate him. He just wants to hear you as well as have you hear from him.

Just try to have a little talk with him, he will listen and answer. Just save some quiet time for him out of your busy schedule, because it is God's breath you're breathing and God's strength that woke you up this morning. Every time God allows you to wake up, he has given you another chance to get it right with him. Tomorrow is not promised to anyone.

Many people plan their whole week and still have not acknowledged the one that helped them make it through the days.

<u>That's My God.</u>

God said, "*Take no thought for tomorrow; for tomorrow will take thought for the things of itself…*" (Matthew 6:34). It is time to spend time with God!

Too often we tend to seek the face of the Lord at our own convenience – when we are feeling down, when we feel like no one cares, when someone dies, or maybe we need an instant answer to a situation. Well, I am here to tell you that God does not work like that. You're either in or you're out. God said in his word "*So because thou art lukewarm, and neither cold nor hot, I will spue thee out of thy mouth*" (Revelation 3:16).

As children of God, we need to make up our minds, God said "*No man can serve two masters: for either he will hate the one, and love the other; or else he will hold to the one, and despise the other. Ye cannot serve God and mammon*" (Matthew 6:24). It is time to get a serious relationship with God.

I know it's easier said than done, believe me I understand. I did not get saved overnight. Once I got sick and tired of being sick and tired, trying to figure things out by myself, seeing that my life was getting worse, and I felt like I was not supposed to be here, I started learning about my salvation and my God. He always seems to step in at the right time.

My friend, that is true! God will make a way out of no way no matter how bad you feel, no matter how bad your past is, God wants you to give it all to him. He is just waiting on you to surrender yourself to him. Let me tell you my friend, when I decided to give my life to the Lord all the heavy weight was lifted off my life. Things started falling in place.

I'm not saying that I have all good days. But when you give your life to the Lord, you will feel different about things that used to bother you. God just wants you to stay humble and let him take care of everything. He already gave his only begotten son for me and you, so don't you think he will continue to do great things? Once you step out the way and let God have his way, you will truly be blessed.

God is so faithful, he will not turn his back on you or leave you alone, he is always awake listening to you, no matter where you are. You could be in the bathroom, bedroom, kitchen, living room or at your job. No matter where you are, God's ears are always open, his arms are always open, and his heart is always open for you. Because God is love.

His love is so sincere that he always watches over his children. Just like a mother does not like to see her child sick or crying because when the child cries the mother's heart is crying also. Just think, God has so much more love for us than we do for our kids!

My friend, stop beating yourself up. You can change and have a closer relationship with God, because he cares very deeply for you and God is a forgiving God. Just like a natural relationship or marriage, it takes time to get closer. I am telling you today my friend, just going through the process that God is taking you through will shape you and mold you to the man or woman of God that he has called for you to be.

Just like baking homemade sugar cookies, first you have to gather all the ingredients together. Then you put all the ingredients in a bowl and blend it real good. When the mixing process is over you got it thick enough so that you can pick the cookie dough up and shape it and mold it to where you want it. Maybe you want mini-cookies or big cookies, whatever. You will have to shape them the way you want them and after the shaping process you have to put them in the oven on the right temperature.

Then you sit and wait for about 20 minutes or maybe longer until they are brown as you desire. After they are done you have to wait another 15 minutes for the cooling process and then they will be ready to eat.

That was a natural example. Here is a spiritual process example. I am going to use myself for this example. Before I truly gave my life to the Lord, I used to smoke cigarettes all the time, I started smoking when I was 23, I used to cough and get pneumonia all the time, but that did not stop me. God help me realize that I was not just affecting myself but my kids as well. They would always ask me when I was going to quit smoking and, I would just avoid answering their questions half of the time.

I have tried to quit smoking numerous times but always failed. At this particular time about 10 years had passed by. I had started going to church and even gave my life to the Lord. I knew I had to do something. I felt deep in my heart that God was working on me over those 10 years.

So, one day, I was smoking, and God really convicted me. It was that time I got down on my knees and cried to the Lord with all my heart and prayed this prayer: "Lord, it is me, Cassandra. I know I have been disobedient and smoked all these years and you even used my kids to warn me and I did not take heed of it." I said, "If you hear me, I am so sorry for ignoring you, please take this taste from out my mouth, Lord please even take the smell of it from under my nose."

I tell you what, once I prayed that prayer; God answered swiftly, even though the enemy tried to make me go back God had other plans.

But the next morning the kids were acting up, my nerves started getting bad, and I had in mind "cigarette time." God's not going to do nothing if I just have one, I thought, so I stepped outside and started looking for someone to pass by with that smoke. I had thrown out the pack I had, just threw them in the trash.

Sure enough, just like God knows you, the devil does, too. So, the first person I saw walking I asked him for a cigarette, and he gave it to me. As I started to pull on that cigarette, I thought I was going to choke to death. I even got sick from the smell. I said, "Lord, that was fast."

However, I realized at that time if I pray and give all my addictions to God, he will take them away. Today I just thank God for his process that brought a change into my life for the better. Life is about change. Either you will change for the better or change for the worse, or you're going to stay right where you are. Ask yourself, "Do I want to stay right here or experience the goodness of the Lord?" It is up to you, friend.

As I mentioned before, it's a process to get fully delivered from the things we are doing and used to do. Those things that are causing us not to walk in the full authority of God are keeping us from getting closer to him.

I'm not saying that you're not close to him now; but God wants us to get out our comfort zone. He wants to make a complete change in us and our lives so that we can spend eternal life with him.

God has a plan for us while we are here on earth. You might not understand your purpose or the reason yet. Only God holds the answers and has the spiritual keys to our future. God has given us spiritual tools to help us through our everyday life's and to help us to know who he really is. You cannot put these keys on a key ring. I am talking about his true living word, The Holy Bible. It gives us directions and our do's and don'ts that will help us to live a prosperous life. Are you ready to make a change in your life and trust God?

Let's get started, First pray this short prayer: "Lord, I have made up my mind. I give my life over to you. Come into my heart and turn me away from my wicked ways. I am ready for a change in my life. Lead me and guide me through the rest of my days. Thank you, Father God, in Jesus name Amen!"

Chapter 4: Get on the Road to Heaven

Now that you have renewed your heart and mind and gave it to God, let your past be your past. All of the guilt and hurt and shame will vanish away. Just leave it in the hands of the Lord, and when trouble creeps in, read these scriptures. They are sure to give you strength and encouragement to help you move forward in the things of God:

➢ *Psalm121:1-3 - I will lift up mine eyes unto the hills, from whence cometh my help My help cometh from the Lord, which made heaven and earth He will not suffer thy foot to be moved: he that keeps thee will not slumber.*

➢ *Deuteronomy 31:6 - Be strong and of a good courage, fear not, nor be in dread of them: for it is the LORD your God, he it is that goeth with thee. He will not fail thee nor forsake thee.*

➢ *Isaiah 41:10 - Fear not, for I am with thee: be not dismayed; for I am thy God; I will strengthen thee, yea, I will help thee, I will uphold thee with the right hand of my righteousness.*

➢ *Zephaniah 3:17 - The LORD thy God in the midst of thee is mighty; he will save, he will rejoice over thee with joy; he will rest in his love, he will joy over thee with singing.*

These scriptures represent the love that God has towards us, his children. God wants us to be happy and to live a prosperous life (III John 1:2), his goal is not for us to be broke and to fail or to be sick. God wants us to walk into the manifestation of his glory; meaning God wants us to walk in the fullness of the fruit of the spirit which is Love, joy, peace, forbearance, kindness, goodness, faithfulness, gentleness and self-control (Galatians 5:22-23).

God is not an author of confusion, but of peace, 1 Corinthians 14:33 tells us. So, when confusion steps in your life, you can be sure it is not of God. All you have to do is ask the Holy Spirit to lead you through each day or any decision that you are making on a daily basis and then wait for an answer.

We always want things in a hurry, God said in Philippians 4:6-8, *"Be anxious for nothing, but in everything by prayer and supplication, with thanksgiving, let your request be made known to God; and the peace of God, which surpasses all understanding, will guard your hearts and minds through Christ Jesus."*

The Peace of God is harmony or agreement with him. When dealing with a hard situation in your life, if you have that peace of God in you, in the midst of the change you will still be calm in your heart. I am not saying as soon as you pray for peace then it will happen suddenly. Just keep praying to God to give you peace and that same person or situation that got to you this go around will not even bother you when God's peace covers you. Just think positive and know that God is changing you from the inside out.

God loves us and he wants the best for us. Once we stop focusing on the things and the cares of this world and focus our love and attention on God, he will show us who we really are and our true purpose here on earth. Because one day we will be no more. Only God's word will stand; God's word will never fade away.

My friend, let's get to know God while he is giving us another chance. If you are reading this book and feel in your heart God is talking to you, please know that he truly is. Gods doesn't always use pillars of smoke or fire to get our attention. Sometimes he uses the simple things to tap us in the shoulder.

God is drawing all his children to him before the end time, my friend. Please do not miss out. This might be our last day here. Just submit yourself to him, trust and depend and know that he is God and Creator of everything. It is not as hard as people make it. It seems so hard for people these days to submit to anything. If God allowed his own son to be hung on the cross for us, we should be able to submit ourselves to him.

It is God who allowed us to get this far in life, knowing that half of the people reading this book should have been dead already from sickness, car accident, heart attacks, etc. God is saying "I am giving you time, my son/daughter. I allowed these things to come up on you to get your attention," and still he is still being ignored.

Chapter 5: Time is Running Out

What else is it that God has to do to prove his love to this world?

Just look back at everything that you had to face, all the tragedies that you had to bear. Who do you think brought you out?

I know for a fact I could not have faced all the things I've faced in my years or gotten through them without the help of the Lord. We as people take God's love for granted too often.

Aren't you glad God's thoughts are not like our thoughts? If they were, all these people who are going around living their lives like they are going to be here forever would have been destroyed long ago. Yes, God could have destroyed them, but something about that GREAT LOVE and COMPASSION he has for us stayed his hand.

My friend, it is time to submit our lives to God. Tomorrow is not promised. Our children, parents, jobs, friends, family, house, cars are not promised for tomorrow. No one knows what tomorrow will bring. As a matter fact we don't know what the next second holds. When God calls us to leave this body, we cannot say, "Hold on, God, let me go back and apologize to this person," or "Just a second, God, I am ready now to give my life to you." It will be too late.

You will hear one of these two things from God when he comes and takes you up.

(1). *"Not everyone that saith unto me, Lord, Lord, shall enter into the kingdom of heaven.....I never knew you: depart from me, ye that work iniquity."* (Matthew 7:21a, 23),

Or...

(2) *"...Well done, thou good and faithful servant: thou hast been faithful over a few things, I will make thee ruler over many things: enter thou into the joy of thy lord."* (Matthew 25: 21).

Which one do you want to hear?

God knows how much we can handle. Often time he takes us through different trials to test our faith in him or to exercise and strengthen that faith, but most of the time we are so hard on ourselves we miss what God is trying to do in our lives. So just examine the situation that you are facing now and ask yourself, is this a test from God to take me higher or is it temptation from the devil? God will never tempt us.

Remember when Jesus first began his ministry, he was tested in the wilderness (Luke 4: 1-13), but only because God allowed it to be. God knew his own agenda, but Jesus didn't. Even though Jesus did not know he was being tested, he never complained, not one time. Just think! Jesus was tempted by Satan for forty days and nights.

Can you just imagine us as children of God being tempted that long by the devil? As weak as we are, we probably would have fallen for Satan's schemes and tricks, trying to make everything that was bad look good. That's how Satan draws us today.

That is why we need to turn to God, because we are no way stronger than Jesus.

That is why God wants us to give him all our problems, because he knows that we alone cannot handle them.

God said he will never leave us nor forsake us (Hebrews 13:5). He has always been there for us, giving us chance after chance, and we are the ones who never acknowledge him while we are trying to take matters in our own hands. It might seem so hard now because we cannot see God, but when you trust him every day no matter what or how you feel or what you are going through, I promise you will begin to feel his presence.

Having faith and praying and studying his word are the ways to successfully get in touch with God. God's Holy Bible is our Bread of Life. Without it, we will starve spiritually.

Try to feed your spirit on a daily basis, even if it is only one or to two scriptures. Read it and mediate on what you have read while you are doing your daily chores, at work, etc. It does not matter where you are,

God promised in Isaiah 26: 3 that He will keep those in perfect peace whose minds are set on him.

Starting today, earn your peace with God by keeping your mind stayed on him and not your problems. Those problems are not really our problems. They are the Lord's concern, so give them to him so that he can fix them. He's always working behind the scenes, even when it feels like he is far, far away from you. He is there. Just stay connected with him.

For example: If you don't pay your light bill, what is going to happen? Your lights will get disconnected, of course. The connection to the source of the power will be interrupted. You have to pay the bill to get reconnected.

Your spiritual power works the same way. So, once you start praying, reading your word and talking to God you will be reconnected to him. That would be called making the spiritual connection. But when we slack off and stop reading and praying to God, the connection will be broken or maybe fade away. If we don't restore that relationship daily with God, we tend to not hear his voice. We let the world crowd him out.

My friend, I am telling you today to stay in prayer for yourself and your loved ones. Let's stay connected to God; it is very important. However, God will not force a connection on you, but he will definitely do it with you. God gives each and every one of us choices; he does not force himself on any one.

There are only two choices you can make: either you're going to serve God or you're going to serve the devil. So many times, we want things to happen right then and there. That is when we make the wrong decisions.

Choices to be made

I remember a time when I wanted a car so bad, to tell you the truth I was not even thinking about praying. At the time, I just wanted a car. I had got tired of walking and begging people for rides. Let me tell you, you sure will find out who your friends really are when you're asking for rides all the time.

Anyways, me being a single young lady, I went car shopping all by myself, like I really knew what I was doing. I drove twenty minutes from home, trying to find a car that I could pay cash money for, because my credit was not so good at that time.

I found a 2004 Gray Cougar. It looked clean on the inside and out. The engine looked brand new. I even test drove the car, and it rode so good! So, I bought it, fixed it up with a sun roof and a radio system. Nobody couldn't tell me nothing at that time.

You know how it is when you brought something with your own money. Made me feel like I had really accomplished something. Me and my kids was not walking no more, no more bumming rides. Can you believe I only paid $2,500.00? I thought it was worth a lot more than that at the time I bought it.

Come to find out about two months later, the car had been in Hurricane Katrina. It had been flooded out, and they just re-did the inside and cleaned up the motor. Looked real good on the outside, but the inside wasn't right. I was driving one night, and the carburetor caught on fire. I thank God I was close to home. No telling what would have happened otherwise.

Like I said before, I didn't pray or nothing about getting a car. I made the decision myself to find a car on my own without consulting God. After that bad experience, I decided the next time I buy a car I will pray and have sense enough to bring a man with me that knows about cars.

I eventually sold that car for less than I paid for it and bought a small car, a Ford Taurus. After a year and half went by, I decided *I am going to try this again*. But this time I made sure to trust and pray to God.

One night I got on my knees and prayed to the Lord and described the car that I wanted. It was not a big detailed description, but I told him that I wanted a car big enough for me and my kids.

I really was not sure how God was going to work this out. My credit was bad, but that night he gave me a vision of what car I was supposed to get. It was a dark blue Chrysler Town/County Van. The next morning when I woke up, I said, "Lead me and guide me which direction to go, Lord, I need a good car."

I felt the Holy Ghost leading me to one particular place. I walked in and ask him if they do trade-in cars? He said, no, they don't normally do trade- ins there. But he told me to give him my information and go look around and see If I can find something on the car lot.

As I was looking around, I saw that Blue Town/County Van that God revealed to me in my dream. I touched it and claimed it to be mine and went back to see the man. He told me that he worked everything up for me and that I had to go the bank and see if I qualified for a loan. When he said that, doubt started creeping in, but I cast it out of my mind.

I said to the man, "God told me it was mine and it shall be."

I went to the bank and the lady ran a credit check. We both were sitting there waiting. I was praying. I asked the lady to come pray with me so we both starting praying. The result came back and said that I qualified for the whole amount. We both said, "Thank you, God!"

I went back with my check and got my car and today I am still driving what God said was mine. It was a lesson well learned. I told you about this experience because I want you to step out on faith today and ask God for something that you been wanting. You may feel that there is no way that it will happen, but just believe. If God did it for me, he will surely do it for you.

Time to make a change

God said, "If you just wait a little while, just talk to me, seek me and wait on me to talk to you, wait on me to make a change in you, wait on me to make your enemies your foot stool, it will all work out."

Don't be so hasty and go forth and do what you feel. Sometimes our feelings get hurt or we get disappointed. God is always present. how can he fix our problem if we are walking ahead of him and trying to do it on our own? Just wait, that is all you have to do is pray and have faith that he is going to do it and thank him in advance for what every you have prayed for.

Don't look at things as they are right now, look beyond that situation, greater things are ahead. We all have a brighter future; but the question is, are you going to allow God to lead you or are you going to walk ahead of him and try to do it yourself? I promise you if you wait on God, everything will work out for you, my friend, because what God has for you is for your best.

Can't no devil in hell change it, because God is a God of his word, he does not break his promises to us. God is the same today, tomorrow and evermore (Hebrews 13:8). He never changes.

If you try to handle the situation yourself, you might as well get ready for disappointment and if it does happen to work out, it won't last for long. Only what we do in and for Christ will last, let him handle it for you.

Often times it seems like every time a person has a made-up mind that they are going to do a certain thing, a distraction always comes and throws them off course. Why is that you ask? Well, two things it could be.

First option, that person really did not in no means have it in their heart to do it in the first place. When I say a person really does not mean it in their heart, I mean they may say out their mouth that they truly love God, but they are only giving lip service. They claim they are sincere about turning their ways to God ways, changing their thoughts and letting God take over their thoughts, but it's just for show.

Lip service to me is when your mouth is moving, and your heart is not registering and agreeing with what you are saying. You continue to do what you want to do without God anywhere in the midst, trying to please people that are around you that at that time.

Remember: God never sleeps, nothing will or can be hidden from God. So many people always trying to figure out ways to keep their hidden secrets from their friends, family, and children not even thinking about God. We as children of God need to be mindful of what we are doing and saying even when no one is around; we should practice on being God-pleasers instead of man-pleasers, God has the power to destroy and man has power over nothing.

The second possibility is maybe they did have it in their heart and God is testing them.

If you really truly mean what you say, that you love the Lord and you will follow his commandments the best way you can until he changes your ways, God knows and will honor that, When you are sincere about the things of God, I believe it makes him smile down on us.

But in order for us to prove our love to God, we have to be tested in sometime in our life. God does not test us to break us down to our weakest point, but be tests us to build us up, to help make us stronger for the next test that comes along. God loves you. He will not put more on us than we can bear (1Corinthians 10:13).

Even though sometimes it seems like he just up and left the scene and here we are trying our best to figure out which direction to take, he's still making a way for us. We're worrying about "how are we going to pay our bills," "where can I look to find a job," "who is going to help me with the kids," "what are we going to eat" and all that time God has gone ahead of us preparing our way. We just have to stand and wait.

I know by experience it is easier said than done. But I am telling you, my friend, just stand still and wait and everything will work out for you. Please don't give up on God and please don't give up on yourself. You can do all things through Christ Jesus that strengthen you (Philippians 4:13).

Without standing on God's words we will never get far in life. Instead of putting your faith and hope on the things that are in this world, which are the things you can see, change your perspective. Put your faith and hope in God and in the things you cannot see. Because faith and hope work together. *"Now faith is the substance of things hoped for, the evidence of things not seen."* (Hebrews 11:1).

Let me give you an example: Me and my four kids lived in the projects in Picayune for about four and half years. About two of those years my kids would ask me, "Mommy, when are going to get a house?" I responded, "I have no idea, because mommy does not have a dime in the bank,"

They would ask me, ask me constantly so one day when my middle son came in the kitchen that evening while I was cooking dinner and asked me, "Mommy, when are we going to get a house? I can't wait to get our new house, our own yard."

So instead of me mentioning about not having no money I just started speaking it into the atmosphere and told my kids, "One day God is going to bless us with a house."

I said, "Lord, I don't know when or how, but I am trusting you for a house." Constantly, me and the kids would pray and speak it in atmosphere.

About a one year later, one of my close friends came by on a Sunday afternoon after church and asked me, "Are you looking for a house?"

I replied. "Yes."

She then handed me a yellow piece of paper and said that her pastor had three flyers for anybody looking for a house. God had dropped me and my kids in her heart to get one of them. It was a flyer about Habitat for Humanity.

I said, "What is that? I have never heard of it in my life."

"It is a group of people and volunteers that come from all over the world to help build houses for different families that are in need of a home to buy," she said.

So, I took the application and went to two different meetings and while I was going through the process, me and my kids were so excited and praying that we would qualify for the house. The enemy kept on throwing stumbling blocks, but me and my kids continued praying and stayed excited about what God had in store for us. They kept on telling me, "Mommy, I just have a feeling this is it."

After a year went by, God blessed us with the house. The most amazing part about it out of 365 people, God allowed me and my four kids to be the second family to pick, and we ended up on the front page of the newspaper.

I thank God for using my kids to first speak it, because while I was looking in the natural and thinking *broke* and seeing no way that I was going to get a house, they had the faith. God had to use my kids to help me to have faith and hope for something that I have never had.

I told you my situation to encourage you. You might have been praying and waiting on God to do something. Just wait a little while longer. It is on the way. Build your faith and hope in God. I know if he did it for me, he will do it for you, but only in his timing. Remember our timing is set different from God's timing, but God is always on time. He is a Loving God!! Just hold on, my friend. Help is on the way.

Chapter 6: Walking in Expectation

My friend, we talked about getting to know God, I also shared a few things that God has allowed me to be used to do and also shared a few scriptures to encourage you. Now let's talk about walking in expectation.

So far after all that we have discussed, your heart and mind should be ready and encouraged enough to walk in expectation now. In Jeremiah 29:11, God said: "For I know the thoughts that I think toward you, saith the Lord, thoughts of peace, and not of evil, to give you an expected end."

What does this mean? God is saying *I know the reason you're going through what you're going through. You don't understand, but I know. That is why you have not lost your mind, that is why you are still here, because I allowed you to face all those things without losing your mind. The reason is I had my hand on you all the time. I told you in my word I am a God of peace and not of evil and I know your thoughts.*

When the enemy had your mind captive, God saw way beyond that and kept you. God knew after you got delivered or came out of the storm you were facing, you would realize that it was him keeping you all along. You would eventually realize that God wants you to walk in expectation.

Expectation is a strong belief that something will happen or be the case in the future. With gaining expectation you must anticipate positive thinking and a positive atmosphere. Be careful and choose your friends wisely, because being around negative people can create a negative atmosphere and God does not work in a negative atmosphere.

Just be very mindful of your choices as well as your words that come out of your mouth. You can either speak blessing or curses in your life (Deuteronomy 30:19) and situations, not only your life but others as well. For example, speaking curses to your situation can prolong the work of the Lord.

When praying and asking God for a car and then turning around and saying that it is not going to happen because you have bad credit, you can cancel the blessing that God already has planned for you. Your faith did not kick in. When a person had doubt, that means they had no deep faith. Therefore, negative things will proceed out of the individual's mouth and will curse the circumstances.

However, you can change your way of thinking into a positive direction and create blessings, so that positive words can proceed out of your mouth and mind. Then God can go head and bless you, because your faith in him will have increased by this time and you will surely live with unexpected gifts from God.

That is God's will for his children he wants us to inherit his riches while we are here on earth and when we spend eternal life with him. If we can just submit to God in all our ways, we will find ourselves satisfied in his Glory instead of looking around and trying to find worldly things.

Don't you want to live with expected blessing coming from the left and right? God will cause your enemies to bless you, leave them scratching their heads in wonder. What a wonderful thought.

He loves you just that much. Don't worry about all those people that seem like they are getting blessed and not living right, because theirs won't last and yours will. Just wait! Your blessings are on the way. Just keep a positive attitude at all times.

Having a Shoulder to Lean On

Choosing a shoulder to lean on could be a hard choice for some people, I know that it was for me. Once a person lets their guard down and trusts people, it seems like you end up getting hurt, lied on.

They will be out there telling what was supposed to be between you and them. They'll be stabbing you in the back. How can a person make the right decision about whose shoulders to lean on when needing a helping hand or something as simple as just needing someone to talk to?

I believe no matter how saved an individual is, God had put someone here on earth that we can talk to. We aren't designed to walk all by ourselves. The point is how do you decide who to trust?

In the Bible, Jesus had his twelve disciples whom he trusted very well in. Out of those twelve best friends, he had one who denied him three times, and another one who betrayed him.

The only thing authorities asked Peter was, "Do you know this man they call Jesus?" His dear friend and disciple said three times, "I do not know this man they called the Son of God (Jesus)."

Even though God had already told Jesus what was going to come to pass, I am pretty sure when Jesus actually heard the voice of Peter saying, "I don't know this man," it hurt him so bad. That is why we should be wise in choosing someone to talk to, first pray and seek the face of the Lord about your situation and if you feel in your heart that God is leading you, then take the next step and trust that God allowed the person in your life and take it from there. One of two things is going to happen.

Number one the person will be in your life just for a season, or number two, God will allow that person to be in your life for a lifetime. It's just a chance we have to take. Remember our thoughts are nothing like God's thoughts.

I remember when God laid on my heart to write this book; I had no idea on how I was going to get started or who was going to help me. When I began to write this book, I stepped way out of my comfort zone. What I mean by stepping out my comfort zone is this: I am the type of person that likes to do plain and simple things myself, without any assistance (help).

But as I started writing this book, God led me to realize, I am going to have to trust someone and get some guidance with this book, because I knew I didn't know anything about writing a book. So, I prayed and asked God to send me somebody to help me because I did not know one person that ever wrote a book here in Picayune. I started looking around on the internet, and asking random people that I saw, and I still could not find anyone. One day I got on my knees and prayed and asked God, to please send me some help, someone with experience.

As I was praying my brother's name came to mind, and I called him. I asked him does he know anybody that writes books and he said, "As a matter of fact, I do. Let me call the man and see if it is ok for you to call."

Within five minutes, my brother called me back and said it was ok, so I called and that's when my journey writing this book came together. I was introduced to Mr. Bill, a true man of God that hears the voice of our father God.

After meeting with Mr. Bill on a weekly basis, we started talking and learning things from each other. Our talks each week helped me to gain wisdom, knowledge and understanding of the things of God that I would have never imagined. God gave me clear vision on what I am supposed to base my book on. I thank God for sending me someone like Mr. Bill to teach me more about the things of God and how to illustrate how to pull my book together. We all could learn things from somebody. Just pray and trust God as he leads you to that special person he has ordained to be in your life.

Always remember having a shoulder to lean on could help you more than you think. I know once I changed my way of thinking and stepped out on faith, God used Mr. Bill to listen and help me to get so far in writing a book, something I would have never accomplish by myself.

There are teachers all over the world. We should stop to listen, observe and give them a chance, because when God is in the midst you cannot go wrong.

However, I am not saying that the first person that comes along is going to be the one. In God's word he said "*Beloved, believe not every spirit, but try the spirit whether they are of God: because many false prophets are gone out into the world.*" (1 John 4:1). The Bible declares that there are many false prophets all over the world claiming to be one of God's children; there are some people also claiming to be your friend and really not, so be careful who you trust to tell your business to.

Learn how to use Wisdom. It is created and formed above and is pure. It brings peace, is gentle, has a willingness to yield, is full of mercy and good fruits, is without partiality and without hypocrisy. My friend I know it is hard sometimes, but the fruit of righteousness is sown in peace by those who make peace.

Pray and pay attention. When confusion comes, depart yourself from their company, because the presence of other people can stop us from going higher in the Lord. My friend, you have worked too long and came too far to be deceived by the enemy. It is now time for you to get what is due to you. The question is, what are you willing to do to get where you need to go to have a prosperous life?

My friends, just hold on a little longer and one day you will say "*I have fought the good fight, I have finished my course, I have kept the faith*" (2 Timothy 4:7). For some of us, it seems like we have been running a long time but stay focused. The more and harder you run the greater the awards are going to be at the end. My friend, I urge you – do not stop in the middle of the race.

Keep praying, keep pressing, keep encouraging yourself and others no matter what it looks like and regardless of how you feel and the situation you are in. Look up and keep the faith and press on, my friend.

I am reminded in God's word that he stated, "*Greater is he that is in you, than he that in the world*" (1 John 4:4b). God is telling you no matter how big the problem is, no matter how bad the sickness is, and no matter what is going on with your children –

He created you,

He knows all about you,

He knows what is going to happen before you do.

There is no problem/situation too hard for God to handle, because he is already in you. All you have to do is submit to him. "*In all thy ways acknowledge him, and he shall direct your paths*" (Proverbs 3: 6).

The world cannot do for you that our father in heaven can do. Just trust him. So often we pray, and we want things to happen right then and there. My friend, I feel like that all the time, but God is trying to take us to a place where we will wait for him and have patience. We just have to work on it on a day-to-day basis. You will get to a point where you see that God is helping you and delivering you and increasing your patience.

Patience is more than just waiting on him to do things for you. When God increases your patience with yourself, patience with your kids, spouse, co-workers and things that used to get you depressed or frustrated, those things will no longer get to you. When you have patience, you will also have a sound mind to recognize what the devil meant as a distraction to get your mind off of God. Patience will help you to get closer to God than ever before.

Remember, my friend, God has promised any weapon formed against you will not and shall not prosper (Isaiah 54: 17), so with that being said, let God help you. I promise you will not go wrong. All you have to do is look where you used to be and look where he has brought you to. You know that if it was not for God's Grace, where would you be?

Some of us walk in places we had no business, but God allowed us to keep our feet to follow him and go tell another lost soul about his goodness. We have said things that hurt people and damage their spirit, but God still gave us a mouth to talk to spread his word. I could go on and on, but what I am saying is without God's Grace on our lives, we would have been ten feet under.

Let's stop taking our lives for granted and focus on the things of God instead of getting caught up on material things. When we leave this earth, there is no way that all the material things we have can come with us, so let's focus on the things that do matter: your soul and your relationship with God.

Live your life carefully from now on. Stop taking the things of God for granted. You still got breath in your body so that means God has chosen to give you another chance take heed his holy spirit.

Only God knows when he is going to call us home. Remember Proverbs 3: 5 - love and trust God with all your heart and don't lean on your own understanding. If we depend on our own understanding, that means we have put a limit on God. Never forget, God's thoughts are greater, more powerful than our thoughts.

Ask yourself, where would you be without him? With Jesus we are complete. Without Jesus in our lives, we are not complete, because God created us.

I remember a time in my life when I felt like the whole world was against me, when I said everything in my life was going wrong. My car was leaking oil, my dryer had an electrical short, my kids were getting in fights at school and got suspended at the last couple days of school year. I had no food, no money to pay bills. My lights got cut off. Friends that said that they would be there for me turned their back on me when I most needed them.

After all this I am still being kept by my God. I thought he must have forgot about me when everyone else did, but he was there all the time waiting on me to lean on him. Instead, I was trying to call my so-called friends and all along the one who was faithful and was here to help me was there with me all along. My God is so powerful, my friend. He is always willing to take care of you, but are you willing to let go and let God have his way in your life?

First Lady Cassandra Peters

First Lady Cassandra Peters and Pastor Jimmy Peters

Committed to the Journey

Chapter 7: Sold Out

What does it mean to be "sold out"? To the world, it means give up your principles. It means something very different to God.

When you are sold out for God you are:

- Completely committed
- Devoted, faithful
- Have no second thoughts about the decision you made
- Willing to go anywhere
- Willing to do anything and give up everything in order to have a more covenant relationship with God.

God wants us to be sold out for him…

No matter the trial…

No matter the outcome…

No matter the delay.

The enemy is always up to no good. He tempted Jesus while he was in the wilderness, weak, hungry and alone (Matthew 4:1-11). If he would go after God's own son, what makes you think your journey here on earth is going to be so easy?

Jesus overcame the temptation. The only thing he had to cling to, to hang on to, was the Word of God. He chose to stand on the Word of God and to speak the Word of God.

We gotta do what Jesus did. He didn't back down, not one time to the enemy. He did not pattycake with the enemy. He didn't just talk positive in the morning. About the time evening came around, the enemy tried him again. Satan even tried to use God's Word against Jesus.

But Jesus knew not just the words of God. He knew the Word, its meaning, its promises and its protections. Out of his mouth was always the Word of his father. Positive words. Powerful words that will refute and confuse the enemy.

God had plans for Jesus. He knew it. God led Jesus to the wilderness on purpose.

Jesus went there to pray. Unexpectedly, in the midst of him praying and fasting, the enemy showed up. Jesus was weak and hungry. The devil thought Jesus was going to back down. He's always shows up when you're weak and alone, just trying to knock us off balance and off focus. The devil doesn't like unity when you really in love with God.

The best time is that one-on-one time with God. The enemy gets mad and wants to interrupt your connection. He'll do everything he can to distract you from God and God's will.

Just do what Jesus did. The more the enemy tried to dress up his lies, the more Jesus used the word of God as it was meant.

> *It is written. Man* (we) *shall not live* (can not live) *by bread alone, but by every word* (not some words) *but by every word that proceedeth* (comes out) *of the mouth of God.* (Matthew 4:4)

God's words release power to overcome any situation that is coming our way or that is already here. There is absolutely nothing too hard for God. Here's the benefit of studying the Word: you reinforce your understanding of God's promises and you fill your spiritual armory with the right weapons to fight the enemy.

Even though Jesus flesh was weak from fasting, the Spirit man got strong. His spiritual armory was full!

Jesus endured a lot. He suffered just for you and me. Jesus knows how it feels to be:

- broken,
- alone,
- weak,
- tired,
- betrayed,
- abused,
- neglected,
- hungry, and
- thirsty.

He even knows the feeling of almost giving up so much more than we can. Jesus even said at one time, *"Father, why have you forsaken me?"* (Matthew 27:46)

Even when you don't feel his presence and you can't see God doing anything in you and in your life or situation, just know this. God allowed Jesus to go in the wilderness and gave him the resources to come out undefeated.

We gotta be sold out for God. No matter who you are, if he brought you to it, He will bring you though and out of it.

Being totally sold out for God

- will open many doors in your life,
- will break curses,
- will let your enemies be at peace with you, and
- will supply fast healing

It makes what the enemy thought was going to kill and destroy make you stronger, more anointed and more powerful. You will be the head and not the tail, first and not last.

God has already proven himself. Now it's time for us to prove our self.

Let's be sold out for Christ

He prayed to God for us. In spite of what he was about to go through, he still prayed to his father for us. John 17: 1-26 contains the powerful prayer that Jesus prayed to God on our behalf.

These words spake Jesus, and lifted up his eyes to heaven, and said, Father, the hour is come; glorify thy Son, that thy Son also may glorify thee:

As thou hast given him power over all flesh, that he should give eternal life to as many as thou hast given him.

And this is life eternal, that they might know thee the only true God, and Jesus Christ, whom thou hast sent.

I have glorified thee on the earth: I have finished the work which thou gavest me to do.

And now, O Father, glorify thou me with thine own self with the glory which I had with thee before the world was.

I have manifested thy name unto the men which thou gavest me out of the world: thine they were, and thou gavest them me; and they have kept thy word.

Now they have known that all things whatsoever thou hast given me are of thee.

For I have given unto them the words which thou gavest me; and they have received them, and have known surely that I came out from thee, and they have believed that thou didst send me.

I pray for them: I pray not for the world, but for them which thou hast given me; for they are thine.

And all mine are thine, and thine are mine; and I am glorified in them.

And now I am no more in the world, but these are in the world, and I come to thee. Holy Father, keep through thine own name those whom thou hast given me, that they may be one, as we are.

While I was with them in the world, I kept them in thy name: those that thou gavest me I have kept, and none of them is lost, but the son of perdition; that the scripture might be fulfilled.

And now come I to thee; and these things I speak in the world, that they might have my joy fulfilled in themselves.

I have given them thy word; and the world hath hated them, because they are not of the world, even as I am not of the world.

I pray not that thou shouldest take them out of the world, but that thou shouldest keep them from the evil.

They are not of the world, even as I am not of the world.

Sanctify them through thy truth: thy word is truth.

As thou hast sent me into the world, even so have I also sent them into the world.

And for their sakes I sanctify myself, that they also might be sanctified through the truth.

Neither pray I for these alone, but for them also which shall believe on me through their word;

That they all may be one; as thou, Father, art in me, and I in thee, that they also may be one in us: that the world may believe that thou hast sent me.

And the glory which thou gavest me I have given them; that they may be one, even as we are one:

I in them, and thou in me, that they may be made perfect in one; and that the world may know that thou hast sent me, and hast loved them, as thou hast loved me.

Father, I will that they also, whom thou hast given me, be with me where I am; that they may behold my glory, which thou hast given me: for thou lovedst me before the foundation of the world.

O righteous Father, the world hath not known thee: but I have known thee, and these have known that thou hast sent me.

And I have declared unto them thy name, and will declare it: that the love wherewith thou hast loved me may be in them, and I in them."

Let's be sold out for God. He deserves all of us: heart, mind, soul, spirit and body.

O how sweet our Father is!

Awesome is he.

Chapter 8: Having a Made-Up Mind

Sometimes in our lives, it seems like trouble is on every hand. It seems like the enemy always peeking in on us.

Wherever we go the enemy is always trying to distract us, kill our purpose, destroy our minds. It could be at work, church, at the grocery store, school and even in our own home. He'll do anything to take us off the course God has set for us, trying to sidetrack us for the real purpose we are here today.

I am so sick of the enemy coming in when he feels like he wants to. I am so tired of him trying to trip me up. It's time for us to pray until we feel the difference within us, until we can rest in God's plan without the enemy's interference.

Prayer is the key, it unlocks all the answers you been waiting for. It opens the channels of communication between your heart and God's heart.

II Chronicles 7: 14 says *"If my people, which are called by my name, shall humble themselves and pray and seek my face, and turn from their wicked ways; then will I hear from heaven and will forgive their sin, and will heal their land."*

That's what I'm looking for - forgiveness and healing and being able to see God's plan.

We are all God's people. We are here on this earth for a reason. One day God decided he was going to call our name in existence. But we were called and made by God, named by God before we were even born.

God knew all along the problems and issues we were going to face and have to endure. He knew all along people were going to walk out of our lives. He knew all along our children was going to go astray, ignoring everything that we have taught them. He knew from the start we would be tempted on every hand.

But God has given us a choice: to either serve him or the devil. And the devil tries awfully hard to bring us to his side of the fence, to make us choose the wrong master.

But if we just humble ourselves--don't panic, don't worry, don't stress ourselves out – and just pray, yield our heart to God, depend on God to bring us into that place where he wants us, empty ourselves out to him and seek him, call on his name, get down on our face to seek his face to worship him, not looking for a handout.

Just think about God and all the things that he has done and already brought us out of, focus on all he gives us. It should be so easy to cry-out to God. Knowing that he is our savior, redeemer, the Great I Am, Alpha and Omega. He is our very own, our friend, father, lawyer, doctor. He's everything you need him to be.

We can call on him anytime of the day, he is never too busy for us, never too distracted. We can just cry out to God with everything in us. Because God wants the Glory.

<u>God wants the Glory!</u>

If we can just turn, give God a chance, get to know God for who he is, transform our own thinking into God's way of thinking, turn from our sinful ways, our wicked ways, wrongdoing, hateful, dishonest and nasty ways, then we are giving him the glory he wants and deserves.

Guess what! As long as we, or should I, say when we get rid of all those sinful ways, I sound like I'm trying to do it on my own. I can't do it alone, but I can with the help of the Holy Ghost!

Don't sell out on God and don't be tricked by the foolish ways and schemes of this crazy world. Everyone is trying to fit in somewhere and trying to leave certain people out. Everyone has a plan of their own for what they want. Each one will have to answer for their actions.

God judges us by our hearts and the love we have for him and others. God is waiting on each one of us at the finish line. Like I said before, are you going to stop running your race or continue to the end and hear those words "Well done, my good and faithful servant. You have fought the good fight."

Then all those prayers we been praying for days, months and years will be answered. God will finally hear us from heaven.

Sin (being dishonest, hateful, hard headed, disobedient- the list goes on) stops God from hearing us and answering our prayers. But once you give up all your wicked ways and give your life totally to Jesus Christ, he will hear us from heaven. He will forgive us of all of our sins and everything that was broken, damaged, delayed, locked up, held up, misplaced will be healed and found and mended back together for his name's sake.

We have a race to run!!!! We are headed to a place, where there is permanent peace, joy, and happiness. There is no more brokenness, no more sorrow, no more pain, no more disappointments, no more sickness, no more addiction, no more loneliness. That place is called Heaven. There is room for each and every one of us. Will you stop running the race or will you continue the race until the end. Jesus is already at the finish line waiting on us.

Let's give God the glory!

Chapter 9: The Word of God Changes Lives

"Blessed is the man that walketh not in the counsel of the ungodly, nor standeth in the way of sinners, nor sitteth in the seat of the scornful. But his delight is in the law of the Lord; and in his law doth he meditate day and night. And he shall be like a tree planted by the rivers of water, that bringeth forth his fruit in his season; his leaf also shall not wither; and whatsoever he doeth shall prosper." (Psalm 1:1-3)

Blessed, happy, loved and holy, pure in heart is the man that does not walk, listen, follow in the counsel, the advice, the ways, direction, information, suggestions, warnings, recommendations of the ungodly. He doesn't pay any attention to the people that don't put God first in their life.

These people feel that they are always right and never wrong, they always have to put others down. They are people you cannot even reason with, these corrupt minded and mean hearted people. They are sinful, evil and wicked, and Godly people avoid them.

Do not take counsel or advice from these evil people, because they just seek for attention and crave for others to fail, while they stand in the spotlight.

Nor should we stand, follow, blend in, attach our ways to be like those sinners, sitting in the seat of the scornful. Those people are waiting for destruction, sickness, depression, oppression, death to hit other lives, thinking they are above the consequences of their actions. All sin will either bring destruction, distraction, sickness or sorrow, and even death. We will never be happy in our sinful ways.

God is love, and He wants good health and prosperity for all of his children in all we do while we are still on this earth. When we follow the law, the commandments of God, our delight, our pleasures, our joy and happiness come from living in the law of the Lord.

I believe God smiles down on us when we stop going our own ways, to follow His rightful ways.

The same way in the natural, we as parents love our children and are happy when they stop doing bad things and follow our advice. Just think of our Father - He is so awesome and forgiving. His heart is so much bigger than ours. How much happier will He be when we come back to His ways.

Lord, give us a heart like yours, God.

When we live by God's law and practice God's law, and His laws become embedded in our hearts, we are actually meditating on his words, day and night. Because we know who we are living for and who we are working for and of course we are, living the ways of the King's laws and commandments.

And as we follow Christ, we all shall be like a tree firmly planted. We will stand, not move or waver in times of trouble, trials, complaints, issues, bad habits or so-called friends and family.

We will be that tree planted by the river of water. Sometimes the water, the river, the current seems to hit so, so hard sometimes, it almost knocks us down and takes our breath away. But it can't do that anymore. After we know who we really are in God and that God has us planted in Him, the river has no power to move us.

God will bring forth good fruits of peace, love, prosperity, joy, gentleness, longsuffering, goodness, faith (Galatians 5:22).

So, when the storms and the doubts come, we will not be moved.

We will also be like leaves, but we will have so much faith in God, when the wind blows in our lives, we won't feel them or doubt Him.

God will allow us to prosper, to succeed in everything we do and put our hands, heart and minds to do. In Jesus it is so. Amen.

Chapter 10: Let's Get to Work

"And he went into the temple, and began to cast out them that sold therein, and them that bought; Saying unto them, It is written, My house is the house of prayer: but ye have made it a den of thieves.

And he taught daily in the temple. But the chief priests and the scribes and the chief of the people sought to destroy him, And could not find what they might do: for all the people were very attentive to hear him.

And it came to pass, that on one of those days, as he taught the people in the temple, and preached the gospel, the chief priests and the scribes came upon him with the elders,

And spake unto him, saying, Tell us, by what authority doest thou these things? or who is he that gave thee this authority?

And he answered and said unto them, I will also ask you one thing; and answer me: The baptism of John, was it from heaven, or of men?

And they reasoned with themselves, saying, If we shall say, From heaven; he will say, Why then believed ye him not?

But and if we say, Of men; all the people will stone us: for they be persuaded that John was a prophet.

And they answered, that they could not tell whence it was.

And Jesus said unto them, Neither tell I you by what authority I do these things.

Then began he to speak to the people this parable; A certain man planted a vineyard, and let it forth to husbandmen, and went into a far country for a long time.

And at the season he sent a servant to the husbandmen, that they should give him of the fruit of the vineyard: but the husbandmen beat him, and sent him away empty.

And again he sent another servant: and they beat him also, and entreated him shamefully, and sent him away empty.

And again he sent a third: and they wounded him also, and cast him out.

Then said the lord of the vineyard, What shall I do? I will send my beloved son: it may be they will reverence him when they see him.

But when the husbandmen saw him, they reasoned among themselves, saying, This is the heir: come, let us kill him, that the inheritance may be ours.

So they cast him out of the vineyard, and killed him. What therefore shall the lord of the vineyard do unto them?

He shall come and destroy these husbandmen, and shall give the vineyard to others. And when they heard it, they said, God forbid." (Luke 19: 45-48 and 20: 1-16)

Jesus went into the Temple (the main church in Jerusalem). People were doing inappropriate things there, selling things and money changing and other bad behaviors. He began to cast them out of the

Temple. He kicked out everyone that was selling things and gambling and dirtying the sanctity of God's house.

While he was cleaning up the Temple, he told them, "It is written, my house is the house of prayer: but ye have made it a den of thieves and entertainment!"

After he finished cleaning out the bad people, he began to teach daily in the Temple. People listened to him, because he was speaking God's truth to them.

But the chief priests (they were in charge of temple worship in Jerusalem), the scribes (the clerks and secretaries) and the elders came in. They were very upset when they saw people listening to what Jesus was teaching instead of what they were saying.

They started questioning Jesus, trying to make him look bad. "Tell us, by what authority do you do these things? Or who is he who gave thee this authority?"

Jesus turned the questions back on them. "I will also ask you one thing: and you answer me: The baptism of John, was it from heaven, or of men?"

They didn't have a quick answer to that question. They put their heads together and started reasoning and whispering to each other. "If we say of men then they will know we are or find out we are liars. But if we say of heaven they will start believing in Jesus, they will know that he really is who he proclaims to be." They were well and truly caught in a bind. Jesus tied them in knots without lifting a finger.

So, they told Jesus, "We can't answer that question."

Jesus said, "Neither will I tell you by what authority I do these things." He may as well have said, "If you can't figure that out, then you can't handle what I would tell you, either.

Jesus turned back around and continued preaching and teaching the people.

In order for the people in the church to understand the message Jesus was bringing, he had to put in a parable, a simple story to teach the lesson. Like so many lessons in the Bible, it is easy to understand, if we'll only take our time, pray, read and research what God is trying to speak and show and teach us through His word. Here is the meaning of the story as God revealed it to me.

God planted a spiritual church, and lent it to preachers, teachers, evangelists, apostles, prophets, bishops, ministers - anyone that was faithful and willing to abide in all the laws of God, people who are willing to live and love Him. He wants leaders who can get into the hearts of the people, to change their lives and lead them closer to Jesus.

God is sitting back. He never leaves us, but sometimes, God sits and watches us. Are we just talking with our mouths or are we in the race with the right kind of heart? Only God really knows the true heart of every individual.

God sat back just for a season relying on us to take care of the business, to keep everything flowing. And trusting us to give Him what was due to Him at the right time.

God has already planted the vineyard. Good ground, good seeds he did plant. Once the seeds were planted, he left it up to the up keepers, the leaders, the ministers, nursery, choir, the whole body of the church to come together and produce good fruits by plowing, weeding, watering, caring, encouraging, feeding, being there to nourish each other until he returns

When the season and harvest time came, the owner God sent three different prophets at three different seasons. God warned Israel over and over again through these prophets that had been sent. Israel beat them, sent them away, treated them shamefully and wounded and cast them out the vineyard.

God only wanted what was due to Him. He planted the people there. The people forsook God and loved evil. But God was so kind enough to warn them of the coming judgement, loving enough to forgive them and give them another chance.

Israel didn't accept the chance. They beat the prophets, sent them away three different times.

Because they didn't want the owner to get what was due to him. They thought they could keep everything for themselves.

God sent His only begotten son to the vineyard. He sent Jesus to set the captives free, to heal the sick, to perform all kinds of miracles. There they were, face to face with Jesus Himself. They even cast <u>Him</u> out of the vineyard and killed Him.

Because the chief priests and scribes and elders were so self-centered and busy worrying about being in charge and worshipped, they were not worrying about true worship of the One they should have been worshipping. They wanted to be the ones with all of the power and authority.

So, they tried to find fault in Jesus. They continually questioned Jesus, "We gotta know who's we are, who we belong to, who you are working for. We don't believe you are who you say you are. Prove it."

How does this apply to us today? If you are reading this, you are part of the vineyard, the church. God has a purpose for you, for each of us. If you have breath in your body, it is time for you to get to work and stop ignoring the warning signs God is sending to his prophets to deliver to us.

Time waits on no one!!

It's time to go to work, to step out in boldness with a pure heart.

Matthew 5:8 says *"Blessed are the pure in heart, for they will see God."*

That means with your whole heart, you will do all you can do to make God smile, you will obey His commandments, you will love even when you don't feel like it. You will step out of yourself and help people instead of tearing them down. You will not let things and thoughts of this world contaminate, pollute, destroy, poison, infect, corrupt your life or heart!

If you push past or don't get involved or stuck in any of these ways and continue to press to the mark, we will see God face to face. You will focus on being a good caretaker in the vineyard and being ready to give God His due in season.

Just like Jesus made it, we can to. We cannot let anything - or anybody - stop us. There is a greater reward ahead. Let's get to work!

If we put nothing in, we will get nothing out at the end. We have to work while it is still day, meaning we need to work while we are still alive and above ground. Because night is coming for every one of us. We cannot waste any more time. It is time to get to work!

Be blessed.

To get to work we need, as a body of Christ to stop disappointing our maker. We have people assigned to our lives and we cannot please God if we are trying to find fault in others. Everyone has sinned and has fallen short of God's glory. You have and I have. But He still loves us and forgives us, and we should remember that when we look at others and are tempted to cut them down.

Let's get to work and get this vineyard growing. God is depending on us. Ready or not He is returning. Let's give God what is due to Him!

Let's get to work!

First Lady Cassandra Peters

A Relationship with God

First Lady Cassandra Peters

Chapter 11: The Lord is My Shepherd

We are all considered God's sheep. A shepherd is a keeper of sheep; therefore, the Lord is our shepherd. If God's presence was with David in Bible days, surely his presence is here with us today. After all, he did say he will never leave nor forsake us.

In the midst of being saturated with his anointing, he makes us to lie down in green pastures, which means when God allows us to lay down in a cool, safe place when facing a hard situation and it seems like there is no escape. By us laying down in those green pastures, we surrender, and we are yielded to the power of God to take control. Our surrender allows us to step into a better place in God, a place in which God will allow our situation to be turned around for the good and he will surely get all the Glory.

I believe that's why David wrote Psalm 23:1-6.

Remember, though:
- David was a child of God, but he was not perfect. After doing some reading, I can see why David wrote the "Lord is my Shepherd" prayer. He needed God's help.
- He committed sin. With Bathsheba, he committed the sins of lust and adultery and he murdered Uriah to cover that sin. He showed his human weakness.
- David needed to repent and receive forgiveness. Beside the still waters, he

confessed his wrongdoing, professing his faith.

David knew all about needing to be restored. His soul ached with the weight of separation from God, so he repented and his fellowship with God was restored, along with his soul. He told the whole story in his prayer.

"The LORD is my shepherd; I shall not want. He maketh me to lie down in green pastures: he leadeth me beside the still waters. He restoreth my soul: he leadeth me in the paths of righteousness for his name's sake. Yea, though I walk through the valley of the shadow of death, I will fear no evil: for thou art with me; thy rod and thy staff they comfort me. Thou preparest a table before me in the presence of mine enemies: thou anointest my head with oil; my cup runneth over. Surely goodness and mercy shall follow me all the days of my life: and I will dwell in the house of the LORD for ever." Psalm 23:1-6

When you are being led beside the still waters, remember this. Even though your situation may seem hard to bear, and your thoughts are running wild on trying to figure out how to work your situation out or how your situation is going to turn out at the end, keep the faith. Being led beside the still waters will surely keep your mind focused and calm. When the water is still, it has no flow or motion to wash you away. When your mind is settled and not worrying, it then gives God something to work with.

So therefore, after all that worrying and complaining, all those sleepless nights, we should rest beside the still water. God then can restore our souls which means he can renew, rebuild, put us back together when we thought we were going to lose our mind, and even fix the broken pieces of our hearts by mending them back together and giving us hope.

And then he will lead us in the paths of righteousness for his name's sake.

We will then have the door open in our lives, our hearts open for God to guide us, show us our way, and to direct us no matter what situation may come. The path, the roadway for our purpose will not be blocked any longer. We will be walking in the purpose of righteousness, free of guilt and sin which God is requiring of us to enter into heaven for his name sake.

Even after you give it all to God you will still have to encourage yourself sometimes. This life journey is not going to be easy. The closer we get to God the harder life will seem. That's why David said: "Yea, though I walk through the shadow of death. I will fear no evil: for thou art with me. Thy rod and thy staff they comfort me."

Even though David was God's man, he was going through many tests. People were out to get him and kill him. He stood for a little while, although in the midst he did stumble and sin. <u>But he came back to God.</u>

Sometimes the pressure seems so heavy in our lives. We don't know if we are going or coming. This is when we are walking through the valley which is low, between uplands, hills or mountains. In that valley of the shadow of death, it seems dark, a feeling of gloom or unhappiness. The shadow is just an invitation to look on the negative side of your situation.

The devil is always working his negative schemes in our everyday lives. He's trying to make us feel like our trial is going to lead to death. But remember if God brought you to it, he will surely bring you through it. Don't be tricked by the image that devil is showing you.

You will make it out of the valley.

Like I said, sometimes we have to encourage our own self.

In the midst of the situation you are facing today say to yourself:

- *I will fear no evil:* which insures you that no weapon formed against you shall prosper. It will not or shall not take you out.
- *For thou art with me*: meaning God is with you at all time, he will never leave nor forsake you. Stay in the race.

- *Thy rod and thy staff they comfort me* which means when you feel like you're going to faint and stop, God's rod and staff will help you stand, will help you walk. Those aids will keep you in a physical ease and freedom from the hurt of the world, and from the affliction and distress of your problems.
- You're going to make it.
- After all the set up from the enemy, all the blocking the paths and walking in the dark valley. You withstood and made it <u>because you are sitting here today</u>.

So, guess what God did in your favor, for your obedience in trusting him:

- *Thou preparest a table before me* (us) *in the presence of mine* (our) *enemies: thou anointest my* (our) *head with oil: my cup runneth over.*
- Which means God is putting together, equipping in advance and getting ready everything which he has promised us. He is setting up a wonderful table before us, in front of us, right before our eyes. In the presence of our enemies. Those people that said you wasn't going to amount to anything, those people that stab you in your back, those people that abuse you and tear down your character with the words that they speak out of their mouths.

We have been "last" long enough. God did say the last shall be first and the first shall be last.

You're first in line this time!!!

- God sees that you are being obedient. He hears your prayers behind closed doors. He loves you just that much. God will reward you openly.
- God has anointed my (our) head with oil; my (our) cup runs over.
- You have favor on your life. God's anointing represents his power upon you. Walk in it. Your cup is now running over. All the troubles and the sets back were for a purpose and they were to make you to be the man or woman you are today. And now your cup is running over. Which means you have more than enough.

No more lacking!

- Surely goodness and mercy shall follow me (us) all the days of my (our) life (lives): And I (we) shall dwell in the house of the Lord forever.
- Which means certainly, of course, no shadow of a doubt about it. Goodness, kindness, virtue and excellence shall, definitely will follow, pursue and overtake me all the days of my life. Which means every single day in my life, as long as I have breath in my body I will, desire and want to dwell, to abide, to reside, live and stay in the house of Lord forever, eternally and always at all times.

"God has everything you need right in front of you, just trust him.'"

Chapter 12: Stay on the Boat

Stay on the boat – God is coming to your rescue!

"And when even was now come, his disciples went down unto the sea, and entered into a ship, and went over the sea toward Capernaum. And it was now dark, and Jesus was not come to them. And the sea arose by reason of a great wind that blew. So when they had rowed about five and twenty or thirty furlongs, they see Jesus walking on the sea, and drawing nigh unto the ship: and they were afraid. But he saith unto them, It is I; be not afraid. Then they willingly received him into the ship: and immediately the ship was at the land whither they went." John 6:16-21

As evening came, Jesus's disciples went down to the sea. How many of you know that at night, in the midnight hour is the time when the enemy tries to creep in? He worms his way into your mind and your thoughts, and the disciples were the same way.

Sometimes it seems like while we are just lying there in the midnight hour we start thinking about our past. We worry over what we would've, could've and should've done or done differently. When the enemy comes in like a flood to destruct our mind, we feel like Jesus's disciples. We are already in this dark place, because it's midnight. All our kids are asleep, friends are asleep. We feel alone and we allow our mind to dwell in that dark place, that confusion. It's hard for us to detect the presence of Jesus when we're focused on the darkness.

During this lonely darkness our boat - meaning our mind, our thoughts and wild imagination - is keeping us so distracted, that we are tossing and turning in the midnight hour. Our fears arise on the devil's prompting just as the sea arose because of the great wind that blew.

Picture yourself being overtaken by your own imaginations and thoughts. The wind was blowing so hard in the sea, it seemed like the more the disciples tried to row the boat the more the wind blew. That's how it is today. The more I dwell and meditate on a situation or problem in my mind and start pondering on it, feeling I have no control, the more I lose control over my mind and actions. I forget who's in charge.

That's when Jesus will step in. As the disciples thought they were going to lose control of the boat, their lives probably flashed before their eyes. Their hearts were already pounding from the struggle against the storm. They looked up and saw Jesus walking on the sea and drawing closer unto the ship and they were afraid.

Jesus caught them off guard. The disciples were so overwhelmed by the strong winds and the waves crashing and the boat shaking, like they were going to all drown in the sea. Their minds were far off from even thinking about Jesus at that moment.

Too often, that's how we are today, saints of God. We know Jesus is triumphant. But when we are facing a tragedy or in a really difficult place in our life, we lose focus. Sometimes our mind seems to leave or forsake us, <u>But God is right there</u>. When it feels like we are at our wits end, like we can't go on, like our life is just about to be over - Jesus will be walking in while the storm is raging in our life. Like he came to his disciples.

Today, God is walking on our sea, standing there with his bright shining light, arms open, drawing us into the ship, calming the storm, turning what the devil meant to overtake us into something to God's glory. But saints of God, we must not be afraid.

Jesus is saying to someone today. *It is I. Be not afraid. It is me that will calm your mind, calm your heart. Give it all over to me and I will make sure the wind won't overtake you.*

As the disciples willingly received Jesus into the ship, we should allow and be willing and receive that what Jesus is doing in our lives will bring us to that land with milk and honey, that wealthy place in Christ.

<u>Please stay on the boat - God is coming to your rescue!</u>

Chapter 13: Are We Born to be Broken?

We all begin life the same way – we are born. The word Born means the activity of birth, the starting point of earthly life.

Some people believe we are born to suffer, to be broken. They expect life will deal harshly with them and they will be damaged, no longer in one piece, smashed, shattered, crushed. Broken means having given up all hope, being in despair, defeated, beaten, not working properly. No matter who you are, we all have dealt and are still dealing with one or more of those things. Life doesn't play nice with us.

The question today is, Are we <u>born</u> to be broken?

Often, we find ourselves in that place of brokenness, of being depressed, oppressed, stress worried, pressed down with the cares of this world. We even lose many nights of sleep, just plain out tired - not from working but from thinking too much.

Are we born to be broken? Is there a solution?

Yes, there is! We can just give it all to God. He gave up his only begotten son Jesus Christ so we could live, and those lives could be stress free.

Are we really born to be broken? Do we as children of God take God's words into consideration. When we get in a broken place in our lives, do we look to the problem or look to him for the solution?

I have come to tell someone today no we are not made or born to be broken. We are made to triumph.

Jesus Christ himself is standing in the gap for us. His word is his promise.

David said in Psalm 147:3, *"He healeth the broken in heart, and bindeth up their wounds."* Whether those wounds come from home or workplace, family or friends, maybe even total strangers, God has promised to heal our hearts and bind our wounds. But he won't do it unless we turn the hurt over to him. He won't interfere against our wishes.

- God will set you free.
- God will mend the broken pieces back together.
- God will bind up, tie, restrain, bandage ever wound that seems hard to bear.
- Keep going to that secret place, so God can fix you. Let's run to God. Only God can give you that fix, that will fix and set you free. The world has nothing to offer.

Remember how Peter put it? *"Casting* (giving) *all your care upon him: for he careth for you."* (1 Peter 5:7) Jesus cared so much that he healed Jairus's daughter, the cripple at Bethesda pool, the man tormented by demons and many, many others who weren't his followers but believed him to be the Son of God. If he cared so much for them, how much more does he care for you, one of his own?

David knew he wasn't strong enough alone. He declared in Psalm 73:26, "*My flesh and my heart faileth: but God is the strength of my heart, and my portion for ever.*"

Our flesh and our hearth faileth us, we cannot even depend on our own self. But God is the strength of our heart and our portion. God is our everything, forever. Once you really tap into God, have an intimate relationship with him, won't no devil in hell break that connection apart. Stay connected.

The woman with an issue of blood for twelve years knew she needed to get connected to him. She pushed through the crowd to touch the hem of Jesus's robe and was healed by that brief touch. Her faith made the connection which healed her. (Matthew 9:20-22)

"*Trust in the Lord with all thine heart, and lean not unto thy own understanding. In all thy ways acknowledge him and he shall direct thy paths.*" Proverbs 3:5-6

Noah acknowledged God's leadership. God directed him to build the ark, load it with animals and his own family and survive the Great Flood. Only by following God's instructions did Noah and his family live. His own understanding could never have prepared him for what was coming.

"But seek ye first the kingdom of God, and his righteousness; and all these things shall be added unto you. Take therefore no thought for the morrow: for the morrow shall take thought for the things of itself. Sufficient unto the day is the evil thereof."
Matthew 6:33-34

Jesus stayed strong and overcame what he had to endure by looking to God and following God's instructions.

God knows everything we need. If we are seeking his kingdom, we will have everything we need. He will provide it.

In Psalm 34:18-19, we have God's promise that *"The LORD is nigh unto them that are of a broken heart; and saveth such as be of a contrite spirit. Many are the afflictions of the righteous: but the LORD delivereth him out of them all."*

The Lord is nigh, near, close, unto them that are of a broken heart: and he saves such as be of a contrite, repentant, regretful, sorry, apologetic, ashamed spirit. Thank God, because Simon Peter denied Jesus three times in the hours leading up to the crucifixion. When he realized what he had done, his heart broke. He was ashamed and repentant, and he was forgiven.

Many are the afflictions, the righteous suffering, distress, trouble, misery, hardship, misfortune, sorrow, even those that are being tormented. Jesus suffered at the hands of human beings and so must we. We are God's righteous children the upright and doing the best we can do. Others will despise us for the way will live or be jealous of us for what we have in God. They will strike out at us. The Lord will deliver us out of all of their attacks. Everything! There is nothing to impossible for God to do.

Isaiah 40:29 assures us that God gives power to the faint, the weak and to them that have no might he increases strength. God will give you strength to push and move forward. You can't do it alone, but you can do it through him.

Psalm 27:14 instructs us to *"Wait on the Lord: be of good courage, and he shall strengthen thine heart. Wait, I say, on the Lord."* Even at the lowest point and darkest hour in our lives, we must have patience enough to wait on the Lord for strength.

Here are some other assurances to encourage you.

Proverbs 18:10: *"The name of the Lord is a strong tower, the righteous runneth to it and is safe."*

Psalm 138:3: *"In the day when I cried thou answeredst me, and strengthenedst me with strength in my soul."*

Psalm 91:7: *"A thousand shall fall at thy side, and ten thousand at thy right hand; but it shall not come nigh thee."*

2 Corinthians 4:8-9: *"We are troubled on every side, yet not distressed; we are perplexed, but not in despair; Persecuted, but not forsaken; cast down, but not destroyed;"*

Acts 16:31: *"And they said, Believe on Lord Jesus Christ and thou shalt be saved, and thy house."*

Ephesians 2:10: *"For we are his workmanship, created in Christ Jesus unto good works, which God hath before ordained that we should walk in them."*

1 John 1:7: *"But if we walk in the light, as he is in the light, we have fellowship one with another, and the blood of Jesus Christ his Son cleanseth us from all sin."*

Matthew 7:7-8: *"Ask, and it shall be given you; seek, and ye shall find; knock, and it shall be opened unto you. For every one that asketh receiveth; and he that seeketh findeth; and to him that knocketh it shall be opened."*

I have come to encourage someone today. We are not born to be broken. We are born to live as Jesus Christ lived.

Stay humble before the Lord. He will grant you every heart desire you have, every petition you have before him.

Be blessed.

Chapter 14: My God is a Healer

The Devil is mad. He is mad because we are still standing

The enemy fights our mind:
- He thought he had us
- He thought he was going to cause us to lose our mind
- He thought our purpose had been aborted. (cancelled, denied)

I've come to tell someone the devil is a liar and the truth is not in him. He lies with every word, every thought he sends out. He wants us to sicken and fall. That hasn't happened for one good reason.

My God is a Healer!
- He healed my mind… (if he did it for me, he will do it for you)
- He heals the body.
- He heals the soul.

We gotta speak life and not death

We might not see what God is up to right now, but he is working overtime on our behalf. He is sending us strength and healing and prosperity.

The Devil is mad. Because we are still standing.

We said we couldn't take it no more…
- Too many bills,
- No money,
- Car acting up,
- Kids acting up,

- Parents acting up,
- Boss acting up,
- Church acting up,
- Everything acting up.

Romans 8: 37 tells us in all these things we are <u>more</u> than conquerors through him that loved us. Through God!

We need to claim that victory and speak life. When we get bowed down in complaining, we are speaking death and the devil loves to hear it.

In every situation we face that seems like it's getting the best of us, we can conquer, we can overcome by the strength and the love that God has for us and inside of us. There is nothing too hard for God. Jesus conquered facing the cross all the way to the end with the strength of God. With the love his father had for him. Just like he loves us. God helped him to stand up to the torture and pain.

I come to tell someone today the Devil is mad we are still standing.

When someone is mad, they do everything they can to get revenge, to hurt you, oppress you, depress you, discourage you, make you feel less important. They just want you miserable, as miserable as they are. Misery loves company, they say.

The devil wants to drag us down until we give up and become blind to the things that God has for us. He wants us to take our eyes off the riches we have through Jesus and to feel poor and lacking.

The devil is a liar and <u>the truth is not in him</u>. Remember that!

We got somewhere to go in God. We got work to do for the kingdom. We can't sit on our do-nothing and do nothing. Get up and get to work for God's kingdom.

Ephesians 6:12 reminds us *"For we wrestle not against flesh and blood, but against principalities, against powers, against the rulers of the darkness of this world, against spiritual wickedness in high places."*

No one is exempt from this. You can have a master's degree, you can have an apostle's degree, sing until the Heavens shake, shake and shout all over the place. We all wrestle, fight, struggle, not against flesh, blood, muscles, tissue and skin. Our flesh has no power. It's too weak to fight.

We are wrestling with demons and spirits. They come together working up different schemes and tactics to keep our minds and life distracted. If they can shift our eyes from looking to God and make us look to other sources (which will always fail us), they can bring us down.

The devil and the demons hate God and hate us too

Of course, we still standing. That is why the enemy is trying its best to destroy and distract our walk and relationship with God.

Every time we go to do good, evil is always lurking around waiting to distract us.
- So, our nerves can get bad,
- So, we can curse,
- So, we can overeat,
- So, we can talk about our sisters and brothers,

- And any other sin they can push us into.

As long as you have breath in your body and are serving God, you will have a hit out for your life. The demons do not want you to make it. They don't want any of us to make it.

But the word of God tells us in Isaiah 54: 17 that *"No weapon that's formed against thee shall prosper:"*

"No weapon" means absolutely nothing. Not physical, not mental, not emotional, not spiritual. If we are in God's will, nothing the devil tries can prosper.

So why do we continue to let our concerns, our problems, other people, money cause us to be distracted? These are only the devil's efforts to keep us weighed down with thoughts that are not like Christ.

That's considered a weapon. A weapon is used against an object or person to cause harm to make them feel weaker than they are. The battle is going on today in the spirit realm. We cannot see it with our natural eyes. But surely, we can feel the weight, the pulling, the pressure and struggle in different situations.

I have come to tell someone today to be encouraged. Whatever situation you are battling with or struggling with it will not prosper or overtake you! The devil is just mad. Because we are still standing. So, he's trying everything he has to take us down.

Just stand on the word of God, the solid ground. The devil can't touch you there.

Keep standing.

Chapter 15: Break Down the Walls

Walking on this life journey has not been easy:

- I've endured suffering, hurting, sickness, and pain.
- I've been embarrassed, misjudged, pushed to the side, looked over, depressed, and suicidal.
- Life has left me broken, feeling alone and out of place, frustrated, and talked about.
- I've been physically, emotionally and sexual abused and shamed.
- I suffered from insecurity, lack of confidence, betrayal, hopelessness, and worthlessness.
- People took advantage of me, talked about me.
- I've been stepped on by the ones that I poured my heart out to, cared for and even gave my last bit of everything.

Life has a way of leaving you feeling empty on the inside. And leaving you with no more trust, hateful, angry, paranoid. It leaves you questioning the next person that says they love you and wondering if it's true. You get all snarled up in deciding on the inside will I let this love in or will I continue to shut it out and stay behind the wall of my past.

Being afraid and having anxiety at just the thought of the walls of my blocked love coming down, I wouldn't let anyone in. The more I meditated on the negative things that ran through my mind the higher the walls got. Not allowing even <u>Jesus</u> to come in.

I didn't realize that the wall can only be built so high, before I cracked, before I lost it all the way.

A voice speaks to my heart and says,

- I didn't build you like this.
- I built you to be more than a conqueror through Christ Jesus.
- I built you not to be defeated.
- The weapons of your war fare are not carnal.
- You are mighty through Christ Jesus.
- You can pull down strong holds and cast down every imagined power that does not line up to the word or the will of God.
- Abide in me and let me abide in you and you are in this world, but not of this world.
- Let me help you break the wall down.
- Where you are weak. I, the Lord said, I will make you strong.

I wrestled within my mind and heart. The thought of being free felt so, so good, but the feeling of anxiety kept coming back.

I kept hearing "BREAK – BREAK - BREAK THE WALL DOWN, YOU CAN DO IT!!!"

It's time for a break through and this kind you have to take by of force and break every strong hold, that has kept you in prison all these years.

Everybody says:

- BREAK DEPRESSION
- BREAK SUICIDE

Breakkkk!!!! They don't always tell you how. Guess what? The Bible does. God laid it out for us.

In Matthew's gospel we read:

> *"Verily I say unto you, Among them that are born of women there hath not risen a greater than John the Baptist: notwithstanding he that is least in the kingdom of heaven is greater than he. And from the days of John the Baptist until now the kingdom of heaven suffereth violence, and the violent take it by force. For all the prophets and the law prophesied until John."* (Matthew 11:11-13)

What does this all mean?

In Matthew's gospel, the words "Kingdom of Heaven" mean the same as Kingdom of God. When we think about a kingdom, we often have in mind a geographical location such as a nation or a state. But kingdoms are more than that, they are also dominions in which the rules of the ruler are obeyed.

When we read that "the Kingdom of Heaven is forcefully advancing" Matthew is saying that God's

Kingdom or dominion is coming on earth. So, this passage doesn't speak about a rebellion in Heaven. Then what does the verse mean?

Scholars are divided over how to translate the Greek word for "forcefully advancing" (biazetai in the Greek). It can mean:

- "to come with violence," "to force," "to crowd into"
- "to suffer violence," "to be treated forcefully"

On the first reading we understand that as God's kingdom breaks into this world it is breaking into the domain of Satan and sin (see Ephesians 2:2). On the second reading we see that the kingdom of heaven suffers as evil powers fight against it.

In both readings the Kingdom of Heaven is described as coming with conflict. However, the way we interpret "forcefully advancing" goes on to influence our understanding of the "forceful men" who "lay hold" of the Kingdom. There are two options for what type of person they are:

- They could be people who wish to do the Kingdom of Heaven harm (such as King Herod who has just imprisoned John the Baptist - see Matthew 11: 12 and 14:3). On this understanding Jesus is saying that God's Kingdom is coming in power and forcing its way into the world but there are many who will oppose and fight against it.

- They could be people who are determined to squeeze or force their way into the Kingdom of Heaven, because they want to take hold of it for themselves.

In the context of what has happened to John the Baptist Jesus is saying that the kingdom of God suffers violence, and violent men seize it. It is also true that the Kingdom of Heaven is forcing its way into the world and forceful men want to crowd into it for themselves.

This second reading implies that the decision to enter the Kingdom of Heaven requires some kind of vigorous and forceful action. When we read Jesus's similar statement recorded in Luke's gospel it appears that this is what is in mind:

"The law and the prophets were until John: since that time the kingdom of God is preached, and every man presseth into it." Luke 16:16

In other words, Jesus is saying that to come into the Kingdom of Heaven requires deliberate, purposeful and determined action. There is no contradiction between the two statements as recorded in Luke and Matthew – they simply explore Jesus' teaching from a different angle. When we take both verses from Matthew and Luke together, we understand that the Kingdom of Heaven does advance into this world with conflict.

There are forces of evil which oppose God's word and His work, and we see violent men working against God and His church in this world. But God's Kingdom is also coming with power and many people are being freed from the power of Satan as they take hold of the good news of Jesus Christ.

Break down the walls and let Jesus in!

Chapter 16: God Hasn't Forgotten Us

> *"How long wilt thou forget me, O LORD? for ever? how long wilt thou hide thy face from me?*
>
> *How long shall I take counsel in my soul, having sorrow in my heart daily? how long shall mine enemy be exalted over me?*
>
> *Consider and hear me, O LORD my God: lighten mine eyes, lest I sleep the sleep of death;*
>
> *Lest mine enemy say, I have prevailed against him; and those that trouble me rejoice when I am moved.*
>
> *But I have trusted in thy mercy; my heart shall rejoice in thy salvation.*
>
> *I will sing unto the LORD, because he hath dealt bountifully with me."*
>
> (Psalm 13:1-6)

Sometimes it seems as though God has forgotten us. It feels like He has stepped away from the scene and looked right over us without noticing us there.

There are times when I feel like my life is going in circles. I wonder, when am I going to stop going around in the circle and make some progress? It seems like I am always at the bottom of the heap in this life. Where is God in those times?

Is God hiding from us or we hiding from Him? Where is He?

Every time I try to do good, it always seems like I'm looked over, taken advantage of, talked about, put down. Something bad always seems to be waiting just around the corner. Why, God, are you hiding your face from me?

How long do I have to sit here all alone and encourage myself? I feel heavy in my heart and I can barely smile most days. Why do I even bother to try?

O God, how long?

It seems like my enemies are winning. They have the upper hand. I know I'm innocent, but I feel so guilty. Why? I'm not sure. Is it because I can't feel You with me?

Will you consider me, God?

Will you listen to me, God and dry my tears away from my eyes? Please come back so I can stop thinking about life ending. Will you come, God? Can you hear me?

When I am sad, and torn, and miserable. my enemy smiles. He is glad to see me broken. He thinks he's won and defeated me. He thinks by defeating me, he's defeating You, too.

But through it all, God, I have trusted You. I've kept looking for You and Your presence.

I'm claiming Your promises. I know that my heart shall rejoice in salvation, freedom, lovingkindness one day. I trust You to keep those promises.

I will sing praises to you, Lord. Because you never let me go, through it all. You were always right there, even when I didn't see You.

God, you did hear my cry! I love you God. Amen!

Chapter 17: How to Really Seek the Face of God

Seeking the very presence of God will help us to have access to God. We will be right in that place where he is. We all know God is omnipresent therefore he is everywhere – his power is ever-present in all things. But are we looking on his face?

Don't you want more of God's presence to fill you, that sweet presence that makes you feel like you're floating? The sweet presence that passes all understanding (Philippians 4:7) and puts a sure feeling in your heart? The knowledge that my God is in control.

Being in the true presence of God will help you forget about yourself and learn to focus and rely on God on whatever you need him to do. Even when things get a little blurry, when it seems the trouble is going to last always, seek his face. Seeking the very presence of God (his face) will bring you such peace and you may be surprised at the results.

Remember God is an on on-time God. He is not coming when we think he should, but he *is* coming. Continue to seek his face.

Everything is coming together just as it was planned by the master God himself.

First Lady Cassandra Peters

First Lady Cassandra Peters in the pulpit

Faithful Obedience to God Makes You a Winner!

Chapter 18: Be Not Afraid!

"Fret not thyself because of evildoers, neither be thou envious against the workers of iniquity.

For they shall soon be cut down like the grass, and wither as the green herb.

Trust in the LORD, and do good; so shalt thou dwell in the land, and verily thou shalt be fed.

Delight thyself also in the LORD: and he shall give thee the desires of thine heart.

Commit thy way unto the LORD; trust also in him; and he shall bring it to pass."

(Psalm 37:1-5)

Don't be afraid of people who want to wrong you and do wrong things to you. Do not be jealous of what they gain with their evil ways. They will try to come and make you feel like you are the one doing wrong. Stand still and watch the hand of God move.

For one day, they will suffer for their mischief and bad ways towards you and others. No matter what happens, lean on and trust in God and always do good. So, you will inherit what God has predestined for you to have while you still have breath in your body.

Both spiritually and naturally, you will be blessed if you just relax, love and trust God. Every dream and desire you ever had in your heart will be fulfilled in His will. He - God - will fulfill just that.

Be faithful to God and give Him every part of your life; trust Him in good and bad times and in all times. He will make all that He said to you come to pass. Amen!!!

Chapter 19: Leaving Carnality, Walking into Reality

Paul wrote to the church at Corinth with a heavy charge.

"And I, brethren, could not speak unto you as unto spiritual, but as carnal, even as unto babes in Christ." I Corinthians 3: 1

He meant they were still living by the flesh. And don't we do the same, living in our own poison, our own pleasures, and appetites, things designed to satisfy us and not to sanctify God.

God gave us milk: The Word to follow, the foundation to stand on and a guide to live by. We have a hard time doing these things because we walk our own path. We want to go our own way.

God didn't go straight to the meat and say, follow my commandments today or you will fall dead today. No, He gave us gentle leadership and directions, He gave His son Jesus Christ's blood, so we can have chance after chance. He gave us baby steps to take so we could come to Him.

But we are letting jealousy, hatred, and division keep us separated Him, blocking us from having a true relationship with God.

It is time for us stop walking in our own carnality and start walking into God's reality!

How many people want the Holy Ghost to move in their lives, but aren't willing to give over control? God's reality is, He will accept no other gods before Him. If you won't give Him control, He will let you go your own way.

Carnality pertains to this flesh or body. It's giving control to our passions, to strong, uncontrollable emotions, pleasures, worldly happiness, enjoyment or appetites. Carnality is a natural desire to satisfy a bodily need especially for food. Whatever you come in contact with - the flesh, our passions, pleasures or appetites – won't satisfy you for long. It only last for a little while.

That leads us to have carnal minds, to keep going back and forth, back and forth, looking for more pleasure or the next thrill. We will never get satisfied and never live the life God has ordained for us to live if we continue to do things our own way. We need to stop letting our flesh control us and start control our flesh.

You might ask, how do we do that? First, you've got to confess where you fall. Go over to 1 John 1: 9. God's word promises, if we confess our sins, he is faithful and just to forgive us our sins, and to cleanse us from all unrighteousness.

We've got to recognize the area we need help in. Tell God all about it, admit to Him how we've strayed. Ask him to forgive us and give us the strength we need to conquer that thing. He will! God is so faithful to His word.

God's word is only here to help direct us to the right path so we can get right with Him.

2 Timothy 3:16 says *"All scripture is given by inspiration of God:"* (each word in the Bible given to us by God gives us the power to overcome anything, if we only believe!!) *"and is profitable for doctrine:"* (these scriptures are valuable and useful in our everyday lives, to teach us the right way to live.)

However, the scriptures are used to reprove us, not to tear us down or make us give up. But to rebuke us to the point we feel guilty going against God word and steer us back on course to Him. He refines us through His word.

God loves us so much and wants the best for each and every one of us. That is why He gave us scriptures: to instruct us on "how to live in righteousness" and "how to be free of sin and guilt," and to correct us in our wrong doings.

God's desire for us is to trust him completely. No matter the trial or sickness, even when we make mistakes., we can depend on Him. Trust God and continue to follow Him listen to his voice.

If we doubt God, it means we don't believe or trust Him. Then we will not hear his voice. Our disbelief disappoints God and He seems to become silent. We can't recognize His voice through all the worldly noise.

John 10:26 *"But ye believe not, because ye are not of my sheep, as I said unto you."*

We got to start putting all our trust in God instead of man. Once we trust God all the way, we will be able to hear His voice and know our Father has spoken to us about our situations. He gave us the answers we had been seeking and searching for.

John 10: 27 *"My sheep hear my voice and I know them, and they follow me."*

Our faith brings us to have a more intimate relationship with God. God promised us he will never leave us nor forsake us.

He has never left us. It's us walking away from Him that puts the distance there.

Jesus even said in John 10:28, *"And I give unto them eternal life: and they shall never perish, neither shall any man pluck them out of my hand."*

God ordained for us to have eternal life, to live forever with him, he doesn't want us to suffer in any type of way. His thoughts toward us are peace and having a sound mind (Jeremiah 29:11).

When we wake-up and keep our mind on God, on not just on things He does for us, but what He offers and promises, what He has given for us – His precious Son, then we keep our focus where it needs to be.

To really, really know the God we serve, our personal Lord and Savior, Jesus Christ, our way maker, our King, our provider, our healer, our mind changer, our mind regulator, our chain breaker, our decision maker, our everything we need him to be gives us an assurance no one can shake. Nobody, I mean absolutely nobody, will be able to change our minds.

We will not and cannot be plucked or snatched out the hands of God. The only way we get out of His hands is to jump out of His reality and leap into carnality. He won't drop us, but He will give us our freedom.

We've got to stay focused on Him and His reality, because if we don't, we will continue walking around with carnal minds, not seeing His path or understanding the things we see or go through. And we will not see our purpose God has for us.

We need to walk – into reality, straight into His loving arms.

We need to see things as they really are in His plan.

We need to know who we are in God.

And know God has a plan for us better and more satisfying than any carnal desire the world can offer.

God just wants us to know, see and recognize who He really is in our lives, who we are in Him. He wants us to totally trust and depend on Him so we can receive the wonderful things He has in store for us.

Chapter 20: Your enemies are trying to set you up (but God has other plans!)

We all know the story about Daniel in the Old Testament.

Daniel was a man who didn't just talk faith. He lived it. Daniel was faithful to God. Even though he was taken off into exile by King Nebuchadnezzar, he kept his faith. Because Daniel had an excellent spirit in him (The Holy Spirit), he prospered in exile. He followed the teachings of his childhood and kept the faith.

He interpreted a dream for King Nebuchadnezzar (Daniel 2) and later a strange inscription for King Belshazzar (Daniel 5). He climbed even higher. Daniel remained an important man in the court through three kings! He rose in authority until King Darius set him over the over the whole realm.

By the time he was serving King Darius, he was a man to be reckoned with. Now anyone with that much power in bound to attract the jealousy of others, and that's just what happened to Daniel (Daniel 6). All of the other administrators and authorities were jealous, so they tried to find something to put up against Daniel. They tried to set him up, they wanted him to look bad in the eyes of his leader, the king.

But they could find no occasion, no mistakes, no sin or nothing that was a fault that made him a bad person. Because he followed God, he didn't stray from the righteous path and his life didn't give them any ammunition to use against him.

They couldn't understand his relationship with God and the blessings Daniel received because of the relationship. So, they had to find something that would maybe make him fall or sin, some type of law that he had broken. Those authorities finally realized: W*e tried to find out everything Daniel has done wrong, but we can't find anything. He serves that God of his. OK, we know that Daniel is faithful to that God he serves. How can we use that against him?*

They decided to change their law. They came up with something to catch Daniel and even went to King Darius for approval. Even though King Darius didn't know the reason why they were adding something to law, he went ahead and approved it. They were so clever and made it sound *real* good. They said all the top people were in favor of it, that the counselors and captains all agreed

The new law that they came up with was: no one could get on their knees to petition or pray or cry out to any God or man except King Darius for thirty days. The king's own vanity played into their little plan.

Mind you, the king and all the princes and administrators knew that Daniel loved God and knew that he got on his knees three times a day to pray to God and give him thanks. Daniel always prayed with his windows open so when he did get on his knees, he could face Jerusalem as he prayed.

Daniel knew what was going on. The same Holy Spirit wisdom that helped him know and interpret the dreams of kings let him understand what those plotters had up their sleeves. That still didn't stop him from getting on his knees praying and thanking God for everything he had done in Daniel's life (Daniel 6: 10). He still prayed three times a day. He was brave and not sneaking doing it either. He still prayed at the open window.

You just know those wicked men already had their eyes on Daniel waiting for him to pray, waiting for him to break the law they made up to catch him. So, when the time came, they ran to King Darius tattling, snitching on him, saying that someone had broken the law.

"You know, King Darius, the new one you signed."

The situation was a set up, but as long as you continue serving the almighty God, no one can harm you. No weapon formed against us can prosper. Daniel kept his faith in God and God kept his relationship with Daniel. Hallelujah!

The jealous officials were finally happy, saying in their hearts, "We finally got him." I'm pretty sure they all had happy faces, thinking, "Now we can get rid of him."

Since Daniel broke their law, the punishment for his "crime" was he had to be cast in the lions' den.

Daniel was faithful, humble and had a great heart, and the king knew. He had a great love and respect for Daniel. I believe his heart broke when he found out it was Daniel that had to be thrown in the lions' den.

The princes knew they were wrong, but they kept nagging at King Darius, saying "remember you signed the petition for the law, no praying to any God or man" (Daniel 6:11).

Then they told him it was Daniel who broke the law. The king felt so bad and sick at heart that he fell for this trick. He tried to think of a way to save Daniel. But the decree was already signed, so he had to go through with it.

The princes saw the look on the king's face and reminded him, "Don't forget, even you cannot change the law. Once the king signs a law, it can't be undone" (Daniel 6:15).

Even in the midst of his pain, King Darius knew the God that Daniel served. King Darius prayed in his heart. He labored all day, praying till the sun went down that Daniel would be delivered unharmed from the lions' den.

That evening King Darius sent for Daniel to be brought and thrown in the lions' den, On Daniel's way to the den, I believe the King whispered to him and said, "Thy God who you serve continually, the one you pray to three times a day, he will deliver you."

Then the den was shut with a big stone. It took a lot of people to put the stone there. The evil princes wanted to make sure Daniel wasn't going to escape the meat-eating lions. They even sealed it with the king's signet and all of their own.

All night, King Darius continued fasting and praying that no harm or danger come to Daniel, that he be delivered out of the lions' den unhurt. He was trusting Daniel's God to do what he couldn't do.

When morning came, the king ran to the lions' den and cried out, calling Daniel's name saying "Daniel, the God that you serve, did he deliver you? Are you still alive? Did the lions eat you?"

Daniel said, "O king, my God sent his angel and hath shut the lions' mouths that they have not hurt me. God found me innocent of wrongdoing and proved that before you I have done no wrong or hurt."

The king was so happy. He had Daniel taken out the den. Daniel believed in God's promise, and no hurt, no bruises or bites were on him

The king had the ones that accused Daniel arrested and thrown in the lions' den, even their children and wives. The lions tore them to pieces, broke all their bones.

King Darius made a new decree. He said if you were even thinking about doing wrong, you better tremble and fear before the God of Daniel. King Darius really now believed that God delivers, rescues, he works signs and wonders in heaven and earth.

God has already prepared a way and place for us his children. The enemy is mad and trying everything he can with every weapon he has to mess-up the plans of God.

Will you be the one to miss the very plan of God? Will you be that one to stop praying and fasting, and pay more attention to your jobs house, friends and money than you do to God's will?

Or will you be the one to let God continue to do what he started in you, no matter which way the enemy shows up and tries to block your path?

It could be in your mind, body, finances, school, kids, spouse or friends. The enemy uses a lot of tools. Will you let the distractions get your mind off God?

God said in Jeremiah 29:11, *"For I know the thoughts I think toward you, thoughts of peace and not of evil, to give you an expected end."* He already knows everything we will face, everything we will go through and everything he will give us in eternity.

So, when Daniel was in the lions' den, God already knew his plan and thoughts toward that very situation. God knew how he would use the evil plans. God shut the mouths of the lions and delivered Daniel out of the pit. He walked out without any bites or bruises, not a scratch.

I believe Daniel slept like a baby in there (that's how much faith he had in the Lord).

Maybe someone reading this feels like they are trapped in the lions' den today and think God is going to let the situation overtake them.

But I've come to tell someone today (maybe you!): God is going to help you overtake your situation. That is the plan of the Lord. And God's plan never fails.

<u>Your enemies are trying to set you up, but God had other plans.</u>

The enemy was trying to set Jesus up in the wilderness but guess what! He stood the test, and the plan of the enemy failed in the end. Jesus held strong to God's word and prevailed (Matthew 4: 1-11).

All the way to the cross, the enemy tortured our Lord Jesus Christ, but guess what!! The enemy was trying to set Jesus up to fail. God had other plans.

They nailed him to the cross, stretched him wide and hung him high. That's why we are still standing today --

because of the love God has for us and the blood he shed for us.

God has a plan for our lives. Trust Him. Just like he brought Daniel through the lions' den, he will bring you through your situation. Remember, God's plan never fails.

Chapter 21: Fiery Furnaces

Let's take a look at Daniel 3:1-30.

We all know the story about the three Hebrew boys, Shadrach, Meshach and Abednego. We've read how Nebuchadnezzar the king of Babylon made an image of gold for the people to bow down and worship (v. 1).

But those three Hebrew boys refused to bow down to an idol god (v. 18). The idol god did not have any powers, couldn't even hear, the idol god did not have life and couldn't even give out blessings.

Who wanted to serve a god like that?

There are still idols today. What can houses, cars, TVs, radio, or people do to help us make it to the Kingdom? Nothing! But we chase them just the same.

The Hebrews boys had a made-up mind: no matter what the king threatens us with, we will not bow down to his gods (idol gods). They believed in something so much more than a statue of gold. They believed in the true and living God. They stood in the knowledge of God's power, trusting Him to make a way for them (v. 17).

When the enemy has plans to tear you down and kill you, God already has plans that you shall live and not die. God always makes a way out of no way. No matter how hot the heat, how difficult the trials and how desperate the circumstance seems. God's near and here to make a way out of no way for you.

Those boys were thrown in the fiery furnace, but they didn't burn. The people watching said they saw not three, but four people in the furnace. They were not alone in the fire.

They came out of that furnace just like they went in. No burns, no injuries, no singed hair. They didn't even smell of smoke!

God surely stood in the gap with the Hebrews. No weapon formed against them could prosper because of faith they had in God.

God will make a way. He will stand with you. Have faith and stand fast.

Chapter 22: Will You Sell Your Birthright for a Quick Fix?

I know we get tired in our bodies and souls sometimes. But that is no excuse to give up on all the promises of God. Anything else we settle for is just a temporary fix.

Esau was a hard-working man. He was hungry at that particular <u>moment</u> when he came in from the hot sun (Genesis 25: 28-34). He'd been working hard in the field, thinking about nothing in particular. Seeing and smelling that pot of pottage Jacob was cooking must have been mighty tempting to convince him give up on his birthright, his possession, his rights to inherit everything his father Isaac was going to give him charge over after Isaac's death. And just because of that quick fix (a bowl of soup, in trade for his birthright) Esau lost everything, his blessings were cut completely off.

Esau was born with all the rights to his father's possessions after Isaac died. He stood to inherit all of the flocks, the tents, the servants, the possessions – everything. But at that moment, the pottage was worth to him more than his birthright. He chose the quick fix for his hunger and gave away his future.

What has our attention today?

I know things are looking just a little blurry. The news isn't good, the world seems to be falling apart. But, my brother, my sister, God's got you. He's got the food for your hunger, the water for your thirst, the peace for your trials. He never fails his own. You've got the eternal answer, so what do you need with a quick fix?

I'm reminded of a humble man, a man who really loved the Lord, a man who obeyed God's every word. Go back and read the book of Daniel. No matter what God said or how strange it sounded, Daniel never second-guessed God. He knew the God he served is the one who created the heavens and the earth, the one who is ruler over everything, every person and every situation. Daniel kept the faith and his love for God never changed. He didn't settle for a quick fix. Daniel was in it for the long haul. God brought him through the trials and troubles and with God's help, Daniel triumphed.

Don't be an Esau, settling for the momentary solution. Strive to be a Daniel, someone who trusts God, believes God's word and looks at the long plan. Don't sell your eternal birthright as a Christian for a quick fix worldly fix.

Chapter 23: The Hand of the Lord is With Us

"Be not afraid of sudden fear, neither of the desolation of the wicked, when it cometh. For the LORD shall be thy confidence, and shall keep thy foot from being taken." (Proverbs 3: 25-26)

Be not afraid, scared, or nervous. Do not draw back and do not give up.

Don't let problems, sickness, people, family, or anything else that works against the will of God take over your life. These things cause fear, anxiety, panic attacks, heart attacks, even heart aches, if you give them any power in your life!

Remember, neither desolation, misery, sadness, unhappiness, sorrow, or depression can stand against God's protection. No distress caused by the wicked, the corrupt things, or the negative things that come our way can overcome His covering.

We as children of God need to take a stand. We must claim and know the God we serve is unmovable and unshakeable. He is ready to throw His mighty protection over us, if we'll let Him.

For the Lord our God shall and will be thy/our confidence, the one we can rely on and trust. He will keep us and stop our foot from moving, our hearts from breaking and our lives being taken advantage

First Lady Cassandra Peters

of. The Lord is with us. How can anything the world threatens stand against us?

Your Place in God's Kingdom

Chapter 24: I (We all) Have a Place in the Kingdom of God

Jesus is teaching his disciples here. This is one of the Beatitudes.

> *"Blessed are ye, when men shall revile you, and shall say all manner of evil against you falsely, for my sake.*
> *Rejoice, and be exceedingly glad: for great is your reward in heaven: for so persecuted they the prophets which were before you."*
> (Matthew 5:11-12)

When you are living and doing the best you can do for God, you are definitely blessed beyond measure, even though people will criticize, condemn, and attack and belittle you, as well as mistreating you. We are running a race where we know the outcome, and we will not be defeated.

We are more than conquerors (Romans 8: 37) through Christ Jesus who is our strength, buckler and refuge (Psalm 18: 2). The false accusations are pushing us closer to our father.

When we were little, if someone talked about us, we ran to mommy or daddy. But in this Christian, spiritual battle we run to God our Father and to Jesus Christ, the one who holds all power in his hand.

When we run to our heavenly daddy, we find strength to be able to move forward rejoicing. When we lean on him, he is very pleased.

We have a great reward and gift in heaven. Hold on, hold on and continue pleasing God and not man. Man will always find fault in us.

The great prophets were truly men of God that walked circumspectly, speaking every word of truth of God. They were all persecuted. So, what better are we? Pray up, fast up and be ready.

The enemy is always walking to and fro seeking who he can make fall and give up and throw in the towel (I Peter 5: 8).

Be encouraged for our great reward is in heaven!

Chapter 25: Heaven is my Home

"While we look not at the things which are seen, but at the things which are not seen: for the things which are seen are temporal: but the things which are not seen are eternal." (II Corinthians 4:18)

While we are standing around waiting on our blessings, things are happening. In the midst of us waiting, praying and fasting, things are happening.

It seems the trouble is on every hand. It seems the trouble is always around. We face our bodies acting up, the church acting up, the car acting up, even the bill collectors acting up. We see these things happening. We hear them happening.

But if we can look past them—even take a peek past them—past the body acting up, the car acting up, the church acting up, the bill collectors acting up, then we can tap into the Spirit realm. When we realize who we are in Christ and who our daddy King Jesus is, we can overcome all the acting up. He is not a failure. He lives in the Spirit and so should we.

We might not see it right now, but our spiritual faith will help us to believe and have no doubt of where we are going.

If my daddy King Jesus tells us, we are the head and not the tail, guess what? I am the head!

Sometimes you have to encourage yourselves. It's good to be encouraging others, But, sometimes you gotta hear yourself speak to your Spirit man, to know you are on the right path.

If my daddy King Jesus tells me I was healed, guess what? I am healed by the blood!

I am a lender and not a borrower. I lend hope to others, I lend encouragement to others, I lend my blessings to others, all by God's provision.

In God, all things are good. He makes my hope come alive. Whatever I lend to others comes back to me with interest from God.

This world holds no good thing. What it offers might look good and feel good for a moment. But it is only temporary, it is only going to last a short period of time. God offers things that are eternal.

Come walking with me on a five-minute journey.

You might not feel like God is near, but I promise you, he is right at hand. God said he will never leave us nor forsake us, no matter what you have done or will do. God won't leave you. God is faithful.

He loves us more than anyone on this whole earth will every care or imagine they care. He always brings us out of the fiery furnace, through the trials and tribulations.

Let's continue to use our spiritual awareness and know that God is taking us to a place called Heaven to worship with him and meet him face to face. No more hurt, no more pain or disappointments. Soon and very soon this journey will be over so we can spend eternity and forever with God.

> *"For we know that if our earthly house of this tabernacle were dissolved, we have a building of God, an house not made with hands, eternal in the heavens".* (II Corinthians 5:1)

We have to know in our hearts that this earth is not our home. Someday, the body that we are in is going back to the dust and dissolve, vanish away, like it never existed.

But while we're here, we have to be living in the Spirit — in spite of our circumstances — and looking past the troubles of this world that comes to steal, kill and destroy us.

We gotta know for fact that God is in control, let him take control of your every thought and motive. Be not just sure, but certain sure.

And know God is working with you, and everything that was meant to be is going to come to pass in his perfect time. No one will ever know the thoughts of God, but we can trust them. God created us. He created a heavenly home with his own hands for us to meet up with him. He is his own designer.

Seek God's face daily. Time spent with him is our daily bread. Be encouraged.

The devil is always up to no good. If he tempted Jesus in the wilderness while he was alone with no one to encourage him (Matthew 4: 1-11), what makes us think that the enemy won't bother us?

When the devil gets after you, things that look good start looking bad and things that look bad start looking good.

We gotta do as Jesus did. He did not back down or bow down to the enemy. The devil is very clever, smart and wise. I tell you this: if you are not covered all the way in the blood, you will get bamboozled, tricked and deceived. Yea, we fall sometimes, when we try to do things in our own human nature instead of relying on God. Let's be wiser to that tricky serpent. He is always up to no good.

God knew he had plans for Jesus. God allowed Jesus to go in the wildness, held him there. Jesus had no awareness of what was about to happen. Jesus was just going to pray for his future plans and work that he was going to do for his daddy. Jesus is a prayer warrior. By fasting and prayer Jesus was preparing himself. He knew he was going to get crucified. He was preparing for the journey.

Like Satan always does, he saw Jesus all by himself in the wilderness and decided to take advantage of the opportunity to tempt God's Son.

He tried everything he could to get Jesus off-focus of the true reason why he was fasting. But when Jesus was fasting there were angels all around him giving him strength and covering him day, night and evening.

I believe that Satan himself tried every trick and scheme. He had wore himself out trying to get to Jesus.

Jesus really endured and suffered a lot. He knows how it feels to be alone. He did not eat for forty days. Of course, he knows what it means to be hungry and weak and be bothered and tempted by Satan.

But guess what? Jesus overcame and conquered it all and so can we. It is time for us to stand strong for our daddy.

Satan is so jealous of God. When Satan got kicked out of Heaven, he took one-third of the angels with him (Revelation 12: 7-9). Satan has power. He can be attractive and tempting. He can lure the unwary.

But his power does not overtake Jesus. If so, Jesus would have failed when he was weak and being tempted in the wilderness.

Our God reigns supreme!

Chapter 26: God wants to do it now!

"And it shall come to pass afterward, that I will pour out my spirit upon all flesh; and your sons and daughters shall prophesy, your old men shall dream dreams, your young men shall see visions." (Joel 2: 28)

God wants to do it now!

He is no respecter of persons, he loves us all the same (Acts 10: 34-35). No one person is more precious to him than another. He created us all.

God called Joel to go warn the people in southern Judah, He wanted them to lay their sin down and stop doing what they were doing. Because of their disobedience, God had sent plagues over the kingdom. He sent palmer worms, locusts, canker worms and caterpillar, fire to burn the grass. An enemy had taken over their land and destroyed everything. Even the animals could find nothing to eat.

God was giving a wakeup call to the land. He wanted them to turn their lives completely over to him and sent Joel to tell them so.

God wants to do it right now!

He warned them that another enemy was coming, another army to defeat them and destroy all that was left. That got the attention of the people.

Then he made a promise: he would restore everything they had lost and more, if they would return to him (Joel 2: 15-27).

God even said, *"For everything that canker worm, palmer, caterpillar has eaten and taken away, I will give you double, even double land. Just turn your life over to me. Trust. Clean yourself up. I will help and I will bless you in many ways"* (Joel 2:26).

God is spirit, and the spirit of man is that part that closely resembles God himself.

The spirit is like the wind and gives man "God-consciousness," awareness of God and his mighty glory. The human spirit is the breath of life which God breathed from himself into us to give us life.

The spirit enables direct communication between God and man. The Holy Spirit gives us assurance of salvation through our human spirit That is why the worship of God is a spiritual matter and never just about flesh. Our spirits worship his spirit, no matter the condition of our flesh. Even a person who is completely paralyzed in the flesh can worship joyously in the spirit.

Any unsaved man has a dead spirit and needs to be born of the spirit of life. Until he receives God's spirit and the blessings he gives, that person is dead and risks remaining dead for all eternity.

God wants to do it right now!

God cares about us. He created us and loves us more than we can understand. God desires for His will to be done in our lives.

We are all precious in his sight and he wants us to be with him for eternity (2 Peter 3: 8-9).

God will provide for us in both spiritual and natural matters if we allow him to pour his holy spirit into us. We must trust and believe what God's Word is telling us. His promises are always kept.

God wants to do it now!

He is waiting for us to come to him. No matter who we are, or what we are doing now or have done in the past, he wants us to come to him. God wants to fill you with the Holy Spirit and bless you with his gifts.

He did not send his spirit to condemn us, or to beat us down, but to give us life (John 14: 15-17, 26; John 15: 26-27). He sent his spirit so we can have help to live right and have a relationship with him for all eternity.

Remember the Lord is that Spirit: And where the spirit of Lord is, there is liberty (II Corinthians 3:17). That means we will be free from depression, free from anxiety, free from bondage, from your past, free from sin and free from the lies the enemy put in your hearts, because those freed by the Lord are completely free (John 8:36). We will be free from everything that has been keeping us from having a real relationship with God

God wants to do it now, today!

It will come to pass only if we invite God into our hearts and let him have control of our spirits.

Amen

Chapter 27: Divine Healing

"And a woman having an issue of blood twelve years, which had spent all her living upon physicians, neither could be healed of any, came behind him, and touched the border of his garment: and immediately her issue of blood stanched.

And Jesus said, Who touched me? When all denied, Peter and they that were with him said, Master, the multitude throng thee and press thee, and sayest thou, Who touched me?

And Jesus said, Somebody hath touched me: for I perceive that virtue is gone out of me.

And when the woman saw that she was not hid, she came trembling, and falling down before him, she declared unto him before all the people for what cause she had touched him, and how she was healed immediately.

And he said unto her, Daughter, be of good comfort: thy faith hath made thee whole; go in peace."

Luke 8:43-48

Here you have a lady that was sick most of her life.

This woman spent her life savings wanting just to be healed, to feel better, to try to live a healthy life like everyone else (v.43). It seemed like the more she went to the doctor to seek a cure, the sicker she got. This lady had the faith that she was going to be healed, but she couldn't find the right doctor, no matter how hard she tried.

Until one day she was in the right place at the right time. A man came passing by. The true and living doctor that held all power in his hands was passing by. He was on his way to the house of Jairus to heal the man's daughter (Luke 8: 41-42).

Just in the nick of time, this lady crossed paths with Jesus. She had lost so much blood that she had to crawl to get to this Doctor Jesus she had heard about him. Her faith was so charged up, it only took one touch at the border, the end, edge of Jesus's garment, just his clothes so her blood flow stopped completely. She was healed.

God made a way out of no way. She couldn't even reach Jesus's hand because of the crowd, but she touched his robe. Because of her faith, she was completely, totally healed (v. 48).

God will always make a way. Have faith and reach out.

Chapter 28: What is the difference between the Soul and Spirit?

The Spirit is the <u>element</u> (part) in <u>humanity</u> (people) which gives us the ability to have an intimate relationship with God.

The Spirit that's inside of us connects to God because God is Spirit Himself.

God is a Spirit: and they that worship him must worship him in Spirit and in Truth (John 4: 24)

Human beings-which is us-are a soul. The word "soul" means light. Whenever the word soul is used, it can mean the whole person

The Bible speaks of our souls in many ways!
• Our soul is eager to sin.
• Humanity is naturally evil, and our souls are <u>tainted</u> (polluted) as a result.
• The life of our soul is removed at the time of our physical death.
• The soul, as with the Spirit, is the center of many spiritual emotional experiences.

"Did not I weep for him whose day was hard? Was not my soul grieved for the needy?" (Job 30:25)

The soul and the Spirit are connected, but separable:

"For the word of God is quick, and powerful, and sharper than any twoedged sword, piercing even to the dividing asunder of soul and spirit, and of the joints and marrow, and is a discerner of the thoughts and intents of the heart." (Hebrews 4:12)

The soul is the essence, the nature of humanity's being. It is who we are.

The Bible speaks of a human soul as being weary and sorrowful. Other descriptions include a thirsty soul, grieved soul, loving soul

It is for the soul of man that Christ died – to redeem him from hell.

The soul joins two worlds, the physical and the spiritual. When a man is saved, his soul keeps the body (lowest) in subjugation to the spirit (highest).

The spirit is the aspect (side) of humanity (people) that connects with God.

The Spirit is like the wind and gives man "God-consciousness" (Ezekiel 37: 5-14). The human spirit is the breath of life which God breathed from himself. His Spirit in me fills me like a cool breath.

God is a spirit (John 4: 24). The spirit of man is that part that most closely resembles God himself. That is why the worship of God is a spiritual matter and never a fleshly consideration.

Every man has a spirit in him (I Corinthians 2: 11). There are four spirits—spirit of man, spirit of the beast (Ecclesiastes 3: 21), the spirit of God, and the spirit of the devil (unclean spirit). Which do you claim for your life?

The spirit of man enables direct communication with God. Without the spirit, we could send up petitions like smoke without knowing God's response. Through the spirit, we can open two-way communication with the Father.

An unsaved man has a dead spirit and needs to be born of the Spirit of life. Only then can the Holy Spirit give us assurance of salvation through our human spirits.

When we die, the spirit goes back to heaven to God who gave it. The soul also leaves the body and is ever alive and either goes to heaven or hell.

God wants us to have the right spirit.

God wants to do it right now!

Chapter 29: The Church in One Accord

It is time for the church to come together in one accord. Not as a bickering, bullying, arguing group but a body in one accord!

I looked up church: It says a group of Christians. That's a good starting point.

The Bible uses the word "assembly" to describe the early church – it means a gathering place, a meeting place, a congregation, a group, a body, come together.

I even looked up one accord: it means to be in agreement. Think of a beautiful choir praising God. The harmony does not come from everyone singing identical notes, but from everyone singing notes which are in agreement.

Church, it is time to get in one accord, pulling together for the Kingdom in agreement with God's goals and wishes.

We cannot get in one accord playing church with our bodies in it, but not our hearts. "Accord" is a package deal. Our body cannot function without our hearts. Our hearts cannot accomplish our God-given tasks without our bodies. We will never fully experience the true living God if our hearts don't turn all the way to God and take our bodies along.

Today, let's experience the true living God as the early church did. Picture the scene. Jesus has been crucified, buried and rose again. He instructed his followers to wait in Jerusalem for God to fulfill His promise of a Comforter. And there they are, waiting.

We read in Acts 2: 1-4:

> *"And when the day of Pentecost was fully come,* (during their spring harvest festival) *they were all with one accord in one place* (one purpose, one mind). *And suddenly there came a sound from heaven, as of a rushing mighty wind and it filled all the house where they were sitting.* (That rushing wind is the Holy Spirit!)
>
> *And there appeared unto them cloven tongues as of fire,* (God's divine presence) *and it sat upon each of them. And they were all filled with the Holy Ghost* (born through the Holy Spirit, spiritually transformed) *and began to speak in other tongues as the Spirit gave them utterance."*

Can you just imagine what will happen when we as Christians get our minds and hearts in one accord with the Holy Spirit, God himself? What a day that will be. We will function as the Body of Christ instead of a bunch of independent bodies. We will work in concert with the Holy Spirit and each other to build the world God created this to be.

If we can just sit our differences aside and stop back biting, judging and putting each other down...if we can come together, I mean really come together with the love of Christ, we can and will experience the same thing as they did. We will truly be in one accord.

There is nothing too hard for God. He can do it. We are the ones that make it so hard to tap in him and his grace.

Let's begin to take this journey we call life seriously. You are either in it for God or you're not. You've got to clean up your life, because God does not and will not dwell in a dirty house. Get your heart clean and he will come right in.

I know it's a process. Give God your all in all. He will help you through the struggle. He will never let you go, even when you fall or fail him. Our God is not a quitter.

Yes, it is time for the church to get on one accord.

Chapter 30: Wait on the Lord!!!

"I will lift up mine eyes unto the hills, from whence cometh my help. My help cometh from the LORD, which made heaven and earth. He will not suffer thy foot to be moved: he that keepeth thee will not slumber. Behold, he that keepeth Israel shall neither slumber nor sleep. The LORD is thy keeper: the LORD is thy shade upon thy right hand. The sun shall not smite thee by day, nor the moon by night. The LORD shall preserve thee from all evil: he shall preserve thy soul. The LORD shall preserve thy going out and thy coming in from this time forth, and even for evermore." (Psalm 121: 1-8, KJV))

<u>I don't want to miss Heaven</u>! God has already prepared a way and a place for us, his children. Will we be the ones to turn away and miss God? Will we keep on doing things our own way and continue to head down the road of destruction? Or will we let God continue to do what he started in our lives? Will we trust him to keep his word?

The Word of the Lord says: <u>*I will life up mine eyes unto the hills, from which cometh my help. My help comes from the Lord, which made Heaven and earth.*</u>

We all have complained about weighing the good and bad. We try to figure out what the outcome of a situation would be and should be – if we do this or that. We want to act for ourselves, solve things ourselves.

It seems so hard sometimes when we say, we should just wait on God. But when we are waiting it seems like either we have plenty of time and he isn't doing anything, or time feels like it might be running out. So, we try to fix things. We try to handle our situation our own selves.

Then we miss what God is really trying to teach and show us in the midst of waiting on Him. There was a lesson there for us and we cut it short or blocked it altogether.

His Word says: He will not suffer thy foot to be moved; he that keepeth thee will not slumber (*sleep or go back on his words*).

God always has a set time and place when he is ready to move in our lives. He works in his time, not ours. He is always right on time.

His Word says: He that keepeth Israel shall neither slumber nor sleep.

Our job, our duty is to just pray, to wait and to know that God is our Healer, Comforter, the Omega, Counselor. He is all we need him to be. He is our all in all and he doesn't sleep on the job.

We should be prepared when God is ready to move in our lives. We can't be ready for his action if we're trying to fix things ourselves. Watching, waiting, praying and believing are what we should be doing, not running around with some spiritual transparent tape and chewing gum. God doesn't perform "duct tape" temporary fixes. He makes eternal repairs!

The Lord is thy keeper. The Lord is thy shade on thy right hand.

We all are in the dress-up room, playing at being spiritual grownups. We might mess up sometimes. In fact, we probably will. Don't dwell on it. Get up, dust yourself off and keep going. Try to do better for his kingdom the next time.

God is coming to get us, flaws and all. He doesn't wait until you're perfect to claim you. He just waits until you claim him to help you get perfect.

The sun shall not smite (*kill or make sick*) thee by day, nor the moon by night.

We don't have to perform perfectly in this world we call our earthly home. He has promised we will be perfect in heaven. He will make us perfect when we get to heaven.

The Lord shall preserve (*protect*) thee from all evil: he shall preserve thy soul.

Your enemies are trying to set you up, but God has other plans. Stay planted in the word of God, keep believing his word and you shall not be moved. No enemy can prosper against you when God is for you!

Do what you can do right now. Love God and every person that he puts in your life. They are there for a reason. No matter how bad they treat you or talk about us, God will use them to his glory.

The Lord shall preserve (*protect*) thy going out and thy coming in from this time forth, and even for ever more.

Your next stop from this earthly home is either Heaven or Hell!! You can wait on the Lord and go to heaven, or rush on your own into hell. Which will it be?

Be Blessed.

Wait on the Lord.

Notes from My Heart

Chapter 31: My Heart is Speaking

God, you made me, I have a purpose.

God, you live in me.

God, you sent me here for a purpose.

God, you came to your own and they didn't even recognize who you really were.

God, help me so I can help others to know that you are real. Especially the ones that don't believe or have given up hope. Help them to really receive you in their hearts for real.

God, I know there is a place for me. A place where people don't look on my outer appearance but get to know me by my loving heart.

Doesn't God open spiritually blind eyes so people can know who is really for you and who's not?

I know tomorrow is not promised but God, what second, minute, hour, day, week are you coming to get me? Please help me to ready, help my heart to be ready when you come. Fill my entire being with your Holy Spirit.

Let your light forever shineth in my heart. (I love you, God.)

Chapter 32: Song of Worship

O Lord, Hallelujah, Hallelujah, Hallelujah, Hallelujah.
You're so worthy, you're so worthy, Lord, you're so
worthy.

O Lord, one day you picked me up when I was down, and
you placed my feet on solid ground,

Lord, I thank you, Lord, I thank you
Lord, I thank you, Lord, I thank you.

O Lord as I look back over my life and think things over,
I see it wasn't as bad as I thought, because God, you
brought me out,

O God you brought me out, and I'm so every grateful to
say
Thank you, Lord, thank you, thank you Lord, thank you.

You save me from this old world.
You didn't have to, but you did.

Lord, I thank you, Lord, I thank you.

Thank you, God, thank you God, thank you.

Let your will be done, God

Chapter 33: Let Your Will Be Done, God

Often times, when we are facing a decision or a problem in our lives, even when loved ones are on their sick bed, we pray and ask God, "Let your will be done."

When we pray and tell God to let His will be done, we are really saying "Lord, whatever it takes. God, I can handle it, I won't give up on you, God, I won't complain. God, I will learn from this. Lord, have your way.

Take a look at what the phrase means, word by word.

Let means: allow to, give permission, to leave to, authorize; or let someone do something while you do nothing.

Your means: belonging to, addressing someone directly.

Will means: a preference in action, to do, must, one deliberately chooses to do, decides upon a course of action, about or going to. Will is also a legal document that tells what a person wants to have done with their property.

Be: exist, happen, occur, take place, come about.

Done: right, correct, acceptable, complete.

Put it together and we are giving God authorization to take His preferred course of action in our lives and acknowledging He will do the right thing for us.

Whatever God does, He does not half do it. He does it all the way and He does it for our good.

About this time in His ministry, Jesus knew what He was going to have to go through for us. His human aspect felt so heavy in His Spirit. He recognized the pain and suffering ahead.

Even then, He didn't say "I don't want to do this." Jesus stated not my will but let your will be done.

He said in Luke 22:42, "*...Father if thou be willing* (if you decide) *remove this cup from me: nevertheless not my will, but, thine be done.*" Right there Jesus also acknowledged it wasn't about him and his will.

As we begin to pray, trusting God for who He is, we gotta wait. The answer might not happen overnight and might nor even happen within a month or years. But in the midst of waiting and being patient, after we've done all we can, and when giving up is not an option, we will inherit the promises of God.

Hebrews 10: 36 says "*For ye have need of patience that, after ye have done the will of God, you might receive the promise.*"

It said might, because God gives us own free will. Either we are going to trust God and let His will be done in our lives or we're going to go about our business and try to do things our own way.

As for me, I want the full promises of God!! I want God's total will to be done in my life.

We need God! We need Him to keep us covered in the midst of life's struggles. If we are letting the will of God be done in our lives, we are already covered.

No Worries!!!

Look back at the Hebrew boys in Daniel 3. Nebuchadnezzar tried to humiliate them into serving their God and a golden statue of himself.

But the Hebrew boys knew the God they served had their backs. They knew they were in the Father's will and whatever was going to happen was the will of God. It had to be done. They knew God had them covered!!!!

They walked into the fiery furnace covered and they came out covered. God never left their side.

So whatever test, trial, situation, problem, habit, issue, heart ache, hurt, sickness, loneliness, whatever you're going through, know that if you are in the will of God and trust Him with everything in you and everything you have, His will is going to be done.

He has you covered.

All you gotta do is give your life totally to him by telling God you surrender, and you give yourself to Him, you give Him your heart. Give up your ways that are not like His ways and turn from your old sinful self.

God will restore everything that should've and could've been yours from the beginning.

Come to Jesus and let His will be done. As long as you have breath in your body you will be ever covered by the blood of Jesus Christ!!!

Read Titus 1: 15-16; 2:1; 2:11-14; 3:2-8

Chapter 34: A letter to God

The reason why I wrote "Transformation" is to help people out there know that you are real, that your works are real, that you are a God of your word, and that you are someone that we can trust and depend on and have faith in and you alone are worthy by yourself. God, I know often time we go through different things in our life's and it seems like we are the only one going through but I know without a shout of doubt that many people are going through the same thing.

As I was writing this book, putting some of my life experiences in here, I was praying that what I wrote will help reach, teach and change someone life out there. I know there is still hope, so I pray, God, that you use me to make a difference in millions of lives by writing "Transformation."

Often time we seem to hold so many things in our hearts because we figure no one will understand us or maybe it is hard to find that certain individual to trust. Well, I am here to let someone know that You are there. You sit high and look low. You can see everything that is going on in our lives and you know all about us.

You are just waiting on us to fully commit to Your will. You and your son Jesus wait for us with open arms.

At times we ourselves make it hard and blame the devil, not knowing the whole time it is us. If we can just change our way of thinking and let go of the past

165

and the negative thoughts and take it to You, letting go of the problems that are troubling our minds, that are keeping us from getting closer to You, our mind will be set free.

We will be free from worries and thoughts that we put in our mind that are not even true, because the more we dwell on a thing in our minds it will form in our hearts and then it will keep our focus on that problem and not on You.

After finishing this book, it has also been inspiration to me all over again seeing how you have used me to work for you over these past years and months and knowing that you are here leading and guiding me on this journey.

I do not take it lightly, God. You will always get the honor and the Glory for all that you are allowing me to do in my life, God.

Chapter 35: This Season has been Approved

"To every thing there is a season, and a time to every purpose under the heaven: A time to be born, and a time to die; a time to plant, and a time to pluck up that which is planted; A time to kill, and a time to heal; a time to break down, and a time to build up; A time to weep, and a time to laugh; a time to mourn, and a time to dance; A time to cast away stones, and a time to gather stones together; a time to embrace, and a time to refrain from embracing; A time to get, and a time to lose; a time to keep, and a time to cast away; A time to rend, and a time to sew; a time to keep silence, and a time to speak; A time to love, and a time to hate; a time of war, and a time of peace." Ecclesiastes 3:1-8

To everything there is a season and a time to every purpose under the heaven. This means to all things there is a proper time, period or term. Also, a time for every plan, goal and every purpose below, beneath and under the heaven.

Saints of God, we live in a world of changes. The seasons seem to go by too quickly or too slowly, but they change. What season are you in today?

Are you in your weeping season? We all go through times of pain where we find ourselves weeping over failed plans, lost loved ones or disappointments. God is there with you in the weeping season, ready to dry your tears. You just have to let him.

Are you in your healing season? Maybe you've been sick or injured or someone has done you wrong. Your illness or pain seemed to last forever, but now you are on the mend, on the road to being whole again. God is there with you, the Great Physician, ready to heal and comfort you as you regain the physical, emotional and spiritual health he designed for you.

Are you in your reaping season? You've worked hard, sacrificed and struggled. Now is the season to reap the rewards of your labors. If you were working according to God's plan for your life, he has blessed your efforts and now you can reap the result of those efforts. God is there with you to celebrate the harvest and honor you as one of the workers in his fields.

What season are you in?

Saints of God, this is not the time to waiver and throw in the towel. God doesn't quit on us and we shouldn't quit on him.

I've come to encourage someone reading this today that this is the season to trust and believe what the Word of God says. No matter how you're feeling. You might be in a lonely season, broke season, heavy burden season, no job season, sickness season or maybe just be between seasons and waiting for the next stage to begin.

Just hold on to God's unchanging hands. He's got you in every season. We're all in different seasons in our lives, but we are all under one heaven and one God.

Saints on God, who are you going to depend on in this season?

Are you going to count on the psychics that claim to read your future? Leviticus 19: 31 warns us *"Regard not them that have familiar spirits, neither seek after wizards, to be defiled by them: I am the LORD your God."* Count on the One who holds your future, not one who claims to see it.

Are you going to count on your so-called friends that come around just to make sure you're still down and not doing better than them? If they aren't in the business of encouraging you, then they are discouraging you and doing the devil's work. You don't need people to tear you down when you have God, who wants to lift you up and make you the best you can be.

Are you going to count on false counselors who try to turn you away from God's word and toward worldly standards? Their season is short and sad. Just look at any newscast or newspaper and read how those worldly counselors fall when their false gods fail them. You serve the one true God who set the stars in motion and cares about every breath you take.

Like I said, Saints of God, it is time to trust God and his sacred Word. The Word of God is a series of books of instruction and laws we must follow in order to make it through this journey. He's given us the roadmap.

In the book of Proverbs 3: 5-6, Solomon writes:

5) *Trust in the Lord with all thine heart; and lean not unto thine own understanding* because your wisdom is not a fraction of God's wisdom. He will never steer you wrong if you'll follow him.

6) *In all thy ways acknowledge him, and he shall direct thy paths* every step of the way, every day of your life. He wants all the best for you and will lead you to it, if you'll only let him. Let go of the worldly GPS and let God set the course. You'll be glad you did.

Saints of God, we just got to realize no matter how hard our lives seem to be at any given season, every purpose, everything that has ever been thrown at us from the time we were babies until now had a purpose and expiration date. It was a season, set by God, and it can't go on beyond that season.

I've come to tell you today you are going to come out of what you been in. Just speak to that season, turn it over to God and it will change. Your words of submission or rebellion bring life or death.

So, let's bring life into that season that it seems like we been stuck in. Turn it over to God. Because according to Romans 8:28, Paul said "*And we know that all things work together for good to them that love God, to them who are called according to his purpose."*

We all have been called, so no matter what season you are in, you will come out in his purpose. Just live according to God's will. Study his word. Spend time in prayer. Submit to his directions. You will thrive in your season.

<u>This season has been approved.</u>

In Conclusion

My purpose, my prayer in sharing this small part of my life and sermons is that lives be changed.

I pray that minds and hearts will be changed. I pray that what was broken deep down inside will be fixed. I pray that you let go of the old and let God have his way in your life to bring his greatness in you.

I pray that faith has increased, and bodies have been healed by some of my testimonies. I pray that you know that you have a brighter future ahead of you than the past behind you.

I pray that God's spiritual wisdom, knowledge and understanding is growing within you so that you can continue to stay in his word and walk with him in your everyday life.

Let go and let God have his way in you and I promise you, God will renew your heart and your mind so therefore when you allow those two things to happen, your life will be brand new and everything that God has promise you will come to pass, but remember my friend it is up to you.

In the name of our father God, his precious son Jesus Christ and the sweet Holy Spirit, Amen!! I am so happy about your future. May God forever bless you.

About the Author

First Lady Cassandra Peters was born into a military family in Honolulu, HI. Reassignment brought her stateside as a young child and she lived in a variety of areas, including Little Rock, Arkansas, Maryland and Mississippi.

As she reached young adulthood, she participated in Job Corps (1994-1997) and worked in several fast food franchises, which gave her a deep insight into customer service. This experience helped her when she became a licensed Certified Nursing Assistant. She has worked in several assisted living facilities over the years, including Mill Creek Rehabilitation Center in Picayune, MS, which led to her experiences as the mentor to a young man working at Winn Dixie.

While attending the Rivers of Living Waters Church in Gulfport, MS, Cassandra felt the callings of ministry and began to pursue learning in that realm. Vision of the Elohim certified her as an Evangelist in 2015. In 2017, she received her certification as an Elder in the organization and by 2018 she had been ordained as a Pastor.

Her commitment to answer God's calling has led her to serve and teach. She and her husband, Pastor Jimmy Peters, met while she was studying and serving. They lead the Peters Memorial Ministries in Poplarville, MS, where they minister to a diverse group of residents of all ages.

First Lady Cassandra Peters

Transformation is Cassandra's first book, as she seeks to share the story of what God has done in her life and can do in yours. Connect with her on Facebook at the Peters Memorial Ministries page.

Index of Verses

First Lady Cassandra Peters

Verse	Chapter	Verse	Chapter
Matthew 16: 24	...1	Psalm 27: 14	...13
Matthew 19: 29	...3	Psalm 34: 18-19	...13
Matthew 25: 21	...5	Psalm 37: 1-5	...18
Matthew 27: 46	...7	Psalm 73: 26	...13
Numbers 23: 19	...1	Psalm 91: 7	...13
Philippians 4: 6-7	...4	Psalm 121: 1-3	...4
Philippians 4: 7	...1, 17	Psalm 121: 1-8	...30
Philippians 4: 13	...1, 3, 5	Psalm 138: 3	...13
Proverbs 3: 5	...3	Psalm 147: 3	...13
Proverbs 3: 5-6	...6, 13, 35	Revelation 3: 16	...3
Proverbs 3: 6	...2	Revelation 12: 7-9	...25
Proverbs 3: 19-20	...1	Romans 3:23	...1
Proverbs 3: 25-26	...23	Romans 8: 28	...35
Proverbs 18: 10	...13	Romans 8: 37	...14, 24
Proverbs 18: 15	...1	Titus 1: 15-16	...33
Psalm 1: 1-3	...9	Titus 2: 1, 11-14	...33
Psalm 13: 1-6	...16	Titus 3: 2-8	...33
Psalm 18: 2	...24	Zephaniah 3: 17	...4
Psalm 23	...11		

www.ingramcontent.com/pod-product-compliance
Lightning Source LLC
LaVergne TN
LVHW041219080426
835508LV00011B/1003